EXCELLENCE
EVERY DAY

More Praise for Lior Arussy's EXCELLENCE EVERY DAY

"When employees take a moment to *make a moment* with customers, excellence happens. In *Excellence Every Day*, Lior Arussy defines the why and outlines the how by which employees can make daily choices resulting in delivering exceptional customer experiences."
—John Moore, author, *Tribal Knowledge*

"Lior Arussy explores 23,000 responses to a global, year-long survey which asks how employees feel their customer interactions have been as compared to the recipients of those interactions. The results are astounding. This is a must-read for companies that want to get the jump on their competition by delivering excellence instead of mediocrity."
—Sheri Greenhaus, Cyber M@rketing Services/CRMXchange.com

"Arussy cuts to the heart of the matter: Excellence is in the eye of the beholder, and customer satisfaction is the benchmark by which every organization should measure their success."
—Greg Gianforte, CEO and Founder, RightNow Technologies

"Random acts of *superior* customer service should not be a fluke or a perfectly aligned circumstance—it should be captured and part of a repeatable interactive process. There has been a power shift to the customer and companies that do not recognize, understand or embrace this shift will continue to gamble with and lose their customer's share of wallet. ... This book is a must-read from the executive level of a company down to the people who actually interact with customers."
—Michael W. Thomas, National President, CRM Association

"*Excellence Every Day* brings a fresh perspective to customer relationships. ... If you want to differentiate your business, read this book."
—Barton J. Goldenberg, author,
CRM in Real Time: Empowering Customer Relationships

"Excellence—as Lior Arussy has rightly defined it in these pages—is one of the few sustainable differentiators in today's economy. The examples and stories in this book are filled with character, vision and wisdom. Drink deeply, and you'll be better equipped to chart a successful course forward—for yourself and your organization."
—Brad Cleveland, President,
International Customer Management Institute (ICMI)

EXCELLENCE
EVERY DAY

MAKE THE DAILY CHOICE—
INSPIRE YOUR EMPLOYEES
AND AMAZE YOUR CUSTOMERS

Lior Arussy

CyberAge Books

Information Today, Inc.
Medford, New Jersey

First Printing, 2008

Excellence Every Day: Make the Daily Choice—Inspire Your Employees and Amaze Your Customers

Library of Congress Cataloging-in-Publication Data

Arussy, Lior.
   Excellence every day : make the daily choice--inspire your employees and amaze your customers / Lior Arussy.
     p. cm.
   ISBN 978-0-910965-79-8
   1. Customer services. 2. Consumer satisfaction. 3. Success in business. 4. Job satisfaction. I. Title.
   HF5415.5.A778 2008
   658.8'12--dc22

2008009170

Printed and bound in the United States of America

President and CEO: Thomas H. Hogan, Sr.
Editor-in-Chief and Publisher: John B. Bryans
Managing Editor: Amy M. Reeve
VP Graphics and Production: M. Heide Dengler
Book Designer: Kara Mia Jalkowski
Cover Designer: Lisa Boccadutre and Dana Stevenson
Copyeditor: Barbara Brynko
Proofreader: Pat Hadley-Miller

Contents

Preface and Acknowledgments xi

Chapter 1: In Search of Excellence? 1

Excellence—Today More Than Ever 3
Excellence or Nothing 7

Chapter 2: The Excellence Myth 9

Admiring the Legends 9
The Culture of Dilbertism 12
The Theory of Excellence 17
Now What? 19
Excellence Every Day? 20
The Excellence Aptitude Test 22

**Chapter 3: Why We Fail to Delight Our Customers
(While We Think We Do)** 25

The Gaps Tell the Story 27
"I Wish I Could Do More" 31

Chapter 4: Excellence—Defining, Believing, Living 33

Excellence vs. Consistency 35

Anticipating Needs 37

Response–Ability 39

The Art of the Human Touch 41

Early in the Morning 43

Sincerely Yours 44

Chapter 5: The Daily Choice You Make— Delivering Excellence One Decision at a Time 47

Choices or Chores? 50

Does It Have to Be Every Day? 51

Twenty Years to Overnight Success 52

Excellence Starts with You 53

The Puzzling Paper Clips 56

Chapter 6: Creating Organizational Excellence 61

Millions of Daily Choices Every Day 61

"You Must Smile Sincerely at All Times" 64

The New "E" 67

Generation Why? 69

Upside-Down Management 71

The Entrepreneurial Manager 73

"We Just Do" 77

Fly the Server 78

Excellence and the Art of Persuasion 80

Chapter 7: Leading Your People to Excellence 83

Serving Your Employees 83

Summer Santa 87

Live in the Customer's Shoes 89

Empowered to Make the Right Decision? 91

Permission to Fail 94

Mistake of the Month 95

Recognizing Excellence 96

Would You Go All the Way? 98

I Will Take the Cynic Over Any Other Employee 100

Tell Me a Story 103

Celebrating the Heroes 104

Excellence Enablement 106

Chapter 8: Making Excellence Personal 109

When I Grow Up I Want to Be 109

Mechanical Performance vs. Impact Performance 113

"How Would I Want to Be Treated If I Were
      on the Receiving End?" 116

Inertia—Falling into a Performance Coma 117

Make It Personal 120

Hey, You! Yes, You! 122

Be Proud of Your Masterpiece 123

It Is All Around Us 125

Chapter 9: Excellence Daily Choice— Personal Leadership 129

Performance at the Moment of Truth 129

In Search of the Right Customer 136

To Tie or Not to Tie: That Is Not the Question 139

Chapter 10: Excellence Daily Choice—
Taking Ownership 143

Waiting at the Altar 143
Chocolate Chips to the Rescue! 145
Never Give Up 147
In Sickness and in Health 150

Chapter 11: Excellence Daily Choice—
Creative Ways to Delight 153

The Extra That Makes the Difference 153
Delighting Customers One Clip at a Time 157
The Old Is Dead—Long Live the Change 160
Creating Customer Compliments in Five Minutes 170

Chapter 12: Excellence Daily Choice—Wow! 173

All You Need Is Love … in 11 Languages 173
Excelling at the Smallest Details 175
The Sweet Taste of Everything 178
A Courier for a Day or Redefining On-Time 178
Who Is Dr. WOW? 180
A Beary Passionate Place to Be 182

Chapter 13: Excellence Daily Choice in Difficult Times . . . 187

Redefining "Getting It Done" 187
With Patience and Perseverance 189
Everyone Listens to Customers 190

Chainsaw and the Art of Amazing Customer Experiences 192
Wrenching Customers Away from the Competition 196
Team Excellence or the Gifts Keep on Coming 198

Chapter 14: Just Imagine ... Then Make It Happen 201

Are You Ready to Deliver Excellence? 204
Lifelong Pursuit of Excellence 206
Only 15 Minutes of Fame? 207
It's Showtime 208
Be Originally You 210
The More You Give, the More You Have 211
I Think I Can 212
Higher and Higher 214

Afterword: Moving Forward 217

About the Author 219

Preface and Acknowledgments

In an ocean of cynicism and entitlement, it's increasingly difficult to find a ray of authenticity and hope. In their absence, excellence will not emerge. Our biggest enemies are not evil intentions or bad actions; the biggest enemy of excellence is simply indifference.

I wrote *Excellence Every Day* as part of my own search for excellence in everyday actions. I was seeking to discover what holds us back from excellent personal and professional performance. More importantly, I was searching for those individuals and organizations that are pursuing excellence despite the naysayers. I was after those people who make the Daily Choice to deliver excellence by focusing on the recipient of their actions. To my pleasant surprise, I found many of them.

This book is dedicated to all those individuals who make the Daily Choice for excellence over mediocrity. It is a love letter of sorts to those who refuse to accept the notion that their work does not really matter. Thank you for enriching us with your excellent actions and choices. You are right. You *can* make a difference. In the struggle between apathy and empathy, you have made a clear choice for the latter. Facing the choice between selfishness and selflessness, you have made a personal commitment to excellence through selflessness.

This book is the result of many people's efforts and commitment, starting with those whose stories are included in this book and who inspired and enriched the message. Thank you all for your actions and inspiration. Keep it going.

In my search for excellence performance in everyday actions, I met and worked with many people who taught me. I am grateful for their formal and informal lessons: Lloyd Wilky, Adrian Paul, Ginny Danforth, Joe Accardi, Karen Wall, Tom Tucker, Howard Camber, Jerry Vass, Bob Elliot, Adam Koffler, Sudhir Murthy, Scott Wilson, Antje Schuett-Fahrenkrog, Ron Moritz, David Holmes, Mike Mueller, Roberto Meir, Juan Carlos Fouz Silva, Anne Csuka, Rich Patterson, Eli Gorovici, Ginger Conlon, Michael Maoz, Doris Biggio, Barry Cik, Yehuda Cik, David Neikrug, Nicole Morgenstern, David Myron, Sheri Greenhouse, Larry Matte, Val Golan, and Harold Ullman. Thank you all.

To Rachel Yurowitz, who believed in this book (as she has believed in many of the projects we've done together so far), thank you for your candid opinions, your support, your professionalism, and, most of all, your friendship. I am not sure how I could survive the storms without you. To Bill Wear for editing and pouring his heart into this manuscript: Thank you. Your insights, comments, and excitement enriched the book in many ways. You live the commitment to excellence in your own actions and it shows.

To David Spindel, Michael Blackmire, and David Swan: Your contributions and support are the building blocks of our joint success. Keep on choosing excellence every day.

To the staff of the Book Publishing Division of Information Today, Inc., including John Bryans, Editor-in-Chief and Publisher, and Amy Reeve, Managing Editor: Thank you.

To my dear wife, Drora, who endures my passion, with all its attendant ups and downs, my deepest gratitude is to you. It seems the journey to excellence is full of mysterious turns. Often, we do not understand until we go through them. Thanks for being there on the journey. To my children, Dalya, Cheli, Liad, and Netnael, you inspire me in so many ways. Be passionate about your pursuits and choose to excel in everything you do. Whether you think you can or you think you cannot, you are right. To my parents and my siblings, you also had to live with the burning passion in me. I am not sure if I should say "I'm sorry" or "Thank you," but I know that you also paid the price.

I often felt as though I was simply writing the book for myself, as a personal guide to excellence and as a reminder of the obstacles that hold me back from reaching the highest level of personal and professional excellence. Among the many lessons I learned on the journey to create the book, one lesson stood out from the rest: Everything matters, and *every* moment is a moment of truth. Be there at the moment of truth; remember the recipient who will live with the results of your actions. Every action matters. Every action has a recipient. Every action will make a difference. And, therefore, every action is an opportunity to elevate your performance to excellence. Make the choice. Make the right choice. There are many people counting on you.

Most of all, remember that excellence is a personal choice. You owe it to yourself.

C HAPTER **1**

In Search of
Excellence?

As I was waiting to check in for a flight on a major U.S. airline, the person in front of me began acting rudely toward the airline representative handling our line. The nature of the problem was not clear to me, but the passenger was screaming and yelling, and, occasionally, I heard a profane word being uttered. The airline representative remained calm and composed, making a conscious decision not to respond in kind. Watching this interaction from a distance, I was amazed by her ability to stay calm despite the customer's repeated verbal assaults. When it was my turn, I smiled and congratulated her for the way she had navigated the storm. "If that happened to me, I would probably have lost my temper and responded to this rude guy in an even ruder fashion," I said encouragingly. She looked at me unmoved and replied dryly, "Don't worry, sir; his luggage is going to Alaska." She then asked if I had any luggage to check—to which I responded with an unequivocal "No," while tightly clutching my bag.

The scene I witnessed at this airline counter is representative of the shift in power taking place in organizations across the spectrum. Individual employees are taking power away from the top executives. In spite of efforts by executives to control brand and the customer experience, excellence is being determined—and delivered—by individuals, on their own terms. In a world where the importance of personal connections is increasingly emphasized, an organization's strength comes directly from its employees who choose to deliver superior performance. Organizational excellence (or lack thereof) is, ultimately, the sum total of the accumulated impact of decisions made every day by individuals. Taken together, these decisions—what I call "Daily Choices"—are the key to an organization's competitiveness and strength.

My experience on line at the airport is a great example of the Daily Choice: At the moment of truth, an employee made a decision that defined the company's success in the eyes of a customer. Every day, millions of similar choices either to deliver superior service or to sustain mediocrity by following generic rules and processes are being made by individuals. It is these millions of daily choices, not corporate strategic decisions, that ultimately account for companies' superior performance and success.

To drive excellence, your organization does not need another top-down strategic plan, but, rather, willing employees who have been given permission to perform. Excellence cannot be mandated from above, it rises from the bottom up. Your employees need to *want* to deliver excellence. So, don't rush to appoint a CEO (Chief Excellence Officer) in your organization; this will not be one of those top-down, enforced activities. At the same time, excellence will not result from the random actions of your employees. (Random acts of excellence will not be sufficient to keep an organization going.)

The roles of organizations and managers will not disappear, but they will evolve in the pursuit of excellence. These changing roles will serve to define and create an environment that encourages employees to choose excellence. Managers need to create an excellence-enabling environment, an environment in which delivering excellence is not the exception to the rule or something in the domain of the "suckers." Enabling excellence will require you to give employees permission to perform. You'll need to provide them with sound information for decision-making, and empower them by granting authority and the freedom to make mistakes.

Excellence—Today More Than Ever

"Capitalism—you basically make people do things they would prefer not to do. You have to have a sort of evil personality to even want to get into that." This is a quote from Scott Adams, the creator of *Dilbert*. Welcome to your employee manifesto!

Why write a book about excellence now, with so many other books available on the topic? A recent search on Amazon.com, using the key word "excellence," resulted in more than 5,400 possible titles. It appears that excellence has been researched and analyzed from every conceivable angle—all that's left is for people to just do it.

But I beg to differ. Judging by the mountain of books and articles on excellence, we should have produced a stampede of excellence enveloping our economy. It's clear that we are nowhere close. Excellence is not a permanent, integral part of our lives. The question is, why not?

Understanding excellence and how to deliver it is at the heart of the matter. We have been captivated by misconceptions and faulty logic that is encapsulated in what I call the "Excellence Myth." The myth presents a paradox: It is precisely the traditional definition of excellence that stops us from achieving our capacity for excellence. The people we admire as legendary—our "excellence heroes," if you will—are holding us back (through no fault of their own). Instead of inspiring us to reach our full potential, the Excellence Myth debilitates us, permitting us to accept something less.

Management consistently diminishes employees' capacity for excellence. In many organizations, willing and motivated employees are squashed by a top-down insistence that procedures are to be followed at all costs. This type of organizational bureaucracy, littered with controlling processes, sends a clear message to employees: Follow and obey rather than take the initiative. "Excellence" is defined as the domain of the rare and few at the top. The rest are expected to remain quiet and keep on marching. Processes have become the primary focus of these organizations, and employees are required to follow them without question. Given such a restrictive environment, it's no wonder that even the most motivated employees are giving up. They are defaulting to playing the obedient soldier while surrendering any initiative or innovation. They do what they are told and try not to think too much. After years of this, how can employees even *consider* the pursuit of excellence? They just want to survive.

Management's eagerness to control everything and everyone has created a new form of employee: obedient, cynical, and devoid of any initiative. The employee's refuge? *Dilbert*, and a descent into "Dilbertism."

Threats from new economies have become the topic of academic research and a multitude of articles. Gloomy reports seem to appear every other day, declaring more job losses to emerging markets with lower cost structures. Asian countries, in particular, are carving a niche in the global economy. Many claim that their successes are the root cause of the decline in new jobs in established markets such as the U.S. But competition is not a new concept to most organizations. We have lived with competition for quite some time. However, it seems that competitive forces have intensified in recent years, accelerated by these new economies seeking their shares of the global marketplace.

Competition has presented us with a simple challenge: excellence or nothing. We live in times where "good enough" simply doesn't cut it anymore. We need every piece of excellence we can gather and every employee's commitment to excellence in order to forge a tough response to the new competitive forces. The new competitors have demonstrated an ambitious spirit and a drive to succeed. While some may not yet have reached a genuine level of excellence, it's clear that the pursuit of excellence is a main focus. We should reflect on why we are losing ground to others, whether they are competitors down the street or across the globe. Are we really willing and ready to compete? Are we pursuing excellence with everything we have, ready to fight back and claim our rightful place? Do we have a fully committed organization, with employees who are dedicated to delivering excellence in order to differentiate our products, services, and experiences—and win the customer's heart in the process? Do our employees have the freedom to get around controlling processes and to make the types of personal choices that will let us rise to the challenge of excellence and win this critical battle?

Sadly, the answer to these questions is "No." With a culture of inaptitude developing among us, created by top-down management and reflected through countless *Dilbert* cartoons, episodes of *The Office*, derisive jokes, and books that tell us to "stop working so hard," we are methodically stripping away our ability to win. In the first decade of the Millennium, as competition has intensified, so has our addiction to cynical content that places us on the fast track to diminished expectations and competitiveness. While some may say, "I'm realistic, not pessimistic," or frame the *Dilbert* attitude as a coping method for stress, it does not dilute the damaging impact of this new direction in our business culture. The harbingers of mediocrity are sending a clear message: "Don't try too hard. After all, what's the point?" "You're working for a moron." "You're helpless." "You're a small screw in a huge machine." "Nothing you do will make a difference, anyway, so you might as well quit trying."

Steeped in this growing "Why bother?" culture, we buy deeper and deeper into the message of our own incompetence and insignificance. The cynicism is affecting our long-term competitiveness. Slowly but surely, one joke at a time, one cartoon at a time, we are ripping away our potential for excellence, committing ourselves to the kingdom of the zombies. We reinforce the message that we are useless and incapable of impacting the big machine we call our organization. After all, it was management that discouraged any initiative and required blind obedience. What *is* the point of striving for excellence, after all? No one will notice, no one will see the difference, and, besides, they don't deserve my best.

Forget about the organization for a minute. Do *you* deserve your best? At the end of the day, if you haven't performed to your potential, you may penalize your boss, but first and foremost, you've penalized yourself. It's your career, your track record, and your reputation on the line.

In light of emerging competitive forces, the market has been flooded with books proposing faster innovation, greater creativity, more intimate relationships with customers, and an entire slew of strategic and tactical solutions to the threat from the global marketplace. I have read many of these books, and one question lingers in my mind: Who will execute these legendary ideas? Who will be there to innovate products or care for customers? Are we talking about the same people? Are we expecting controlling, process-centric managers to allow this type of performance? Are we expecting employees who are afflicted by Dilbertism to go and create excellence that makes a difference?

This intensified competitive landscape requires employees and organizations to be at the top of their game—to genuinely care about the customer and to deliver innovation and distinguished service. In short, it requires us to achieve excellence. "Consistency" doesn't provide differentiation anymore. Consistency is necessary, but it's insufficient. Consistency is far from interesting; if that's all we're offering, customers are likely to seek more exciting options at a competitor's store. The new reality is that organizations today need to be at peak performance all the time. To achieve this, they can only depend on one thing: employee excellence. We need all the innovation, creativity, and risk taking we can muster. But we can't get any of this from top-down, executive-mandated decisions. The decisions must come from the employees themselves.

Excellence or Nothing

Excellence or nothing is the survival choice of every organization or individual today. "Good enough" and consistency are simply not going to cut it anymore. Achieving excellence is our only chance for growth and success.

I wrote *Excellence Every Day* as a wake-up call and as an invitation. As a wake-up call, it warns of danger: Inaction is a self-defeating state that results in miserable mediocrity. It has greater negative impact on each and every one of us than most of us are willing to recognize or accept.

The book is also my personal invitation to you to choose excellence every day. With each new day, we are given opportunities to make conscious choices for either mediocrity or excellence. Any time we choose mediocrity, we get further away from competitive advantage and the chance to win in the marketplace. Each choice should be viewed as an opportunity for organizations *and* individuals to unleash our abilities to maximize performance, to be competitive, to win in the marketplace, and to be the best we can be. Today, more than ever, every personal choice counts. Every Daily Choice for excellence increases our overall excellence capacity. Each employee's Daily Choices impact the sum total of choices contributing to an organization's excellence and competitiveness.

Because the competitive battleground is in the trenches and not at the top, every employee's choice for excellence matters. Together, millions of Daily Choices for excellence made by an organization's employees can create an amazing differentiation and a huge competitive advantage.

It's time to abolish the corporate culture characterized by *Dilbert*-style messages; this culture is damaging our productivity and competitiveness. It is time to empower every employee to make the Daily Choice for excellence. Managers need to shift from a focus on process to a focus on enabling employee excellence. By giving employees permission to perform, managers allow employees to unleash their excellence capacity and make a difference.

We urgently need to regain our capacity for excellence and deliver it every day. We need to dispel the Excellence Myth and redefine excellence as positive, thoughtful, everyday action that is capable of being delivered by each and every person at any time. In doing so, we must defy the misconception that excellence is once-in-a-lifetime achievement that is the domain of the rare and the few. We must make excellence a personal matter and define it as a personal commitment. We must make the Daily Choice every day and execute excellence in everything we do. To get started, we must work to bury the Excellence Myth and to regain an attitude of aptitude. The myths and obstacles we may encounter on our path to excellence will be discussed in upcoming chapters. But in Chapter 2 I'll show how a faulty definition of excellence can cause individuals and organizations to miss the mark when it comes to meeting and exceeding customer expectations. Self-centric definitions of excellence can place organizations and customers on completely different paths that are not destined to meet. As a result, individuals often miss opportunities to perform to their excellence potential, and organizations fail to remain competitive.

Excellence or nothing is the choice we face every day. Only when we learn to make a *conscious* choice for excellence will we stand a chance of winning.

CHAPTER 2

The Excellence Myth

Admiring the Legends

Lance Armstrong	Abraham Lincoln
Leonardo da Vinci	Mozart
Bob Dylan	Paul Newman
Albert Einstein	Rosa Parks
Duke Ellington	Luciano Pavarotti
Al Gore	Pablo Picasso
Katharine Hepburn	Elvis Presley
Alfred Hitchcock	Martin Scorcese
Michael Jordan	William Shakespeare
Martin Luther King, Jr.	Mother Teresa
Stephen King	Oprah Winfrey
John Lennon	Tiger Woods

We all have our excellence icons, and no doubt your list looks very different from this one. Who are *your* symbols of excellence? Who are the legendary individuals whose performance inspires you to reach higher? Whether from sports, science, the arts, politics, or history—whom do *you* put on a pedestal and admire for the excellence of his or her achievements?

In the business world, we have embraced our own legends and symbols of corporate excellence. Many of us watch with awe and admiration at the performance of firms such as Southwest Airlines, Starbucks, Jet Blue, GE, Dell, Google, and the Ritz Carlton Hotels. We are amazed by their phenomenal success. Deep down, we wish we could be like them, but we're convinced that's impossible. They appear to be invincible—champions in a brutally competitive arena, capable of meeting any challenge or problem. Each has reached a level of achievement that is almost beyond our comprehension, and that's where the problem starts.

Many people portray excellence as a heroic, once-in-a-lifetime achievement. It's a privilege reserved for the rare and the few—and, by the way, we don't happen to be one of them. We often view climbing Mount Everest or Olympic competitions with great reverence and consider them pinnacles of excellence. Since none of us is planning to climb Everest anytime soon or is qualified to compete in the next Olympic Games, these actions and events remain the territory of "crazy" people, a territory where we do not belong. These crazy people are capable of crazy achievements. They are not exactly normal, and their willingness to put so much at stake to reach their objectives is not something we can fully comprehend or relate to, let alone reproduce. These crazy people are not *us*. And we are not ready to be them.

The result of associating heroic events with excellence is that we remove ourselves from the field upon which excellence performance thrives. It leads us to conclude that we are not capable of delivering excellence, since we are not ready, able, and willing to subject ourselves to the sacrifices and difficulties such heroic efforts require. They can do it, but we cannot. They are willing to endure it, we aren't. We are not built to endure the sacrifices required for such achievements.

Welcome to the Excellence Myth, where our very symbols of excellence hold us back from achieving it. What a paradox!

We are, in fact, captives of a myth that will not allow us to carry ourselves to the highest possible level of performance. We've created such a high standard of excellence (e.g., winning the Masters Tournament for three consecutive years or flying around the world in a hot air balloon) that we give up on our dreams before we've even made the effort. We dismiss our own potential. We get caught up in the "action hero" definition of excellence that permeates popular culture. This does not result in action, but rather, in inaction. We just stand there and stare, effectively reducing excellence to a spectator sport.

Another dimension of the Excellence Myth is celebrity culture. Following and admiring celebrities—the new legends—has became a science and an art, and, of course, a multibillion-dollar business. From tabloids to books and from dolls to clothing lines, we will purchase our new legend's anointed products and feel that we are somehow part of their world, when, in fact, we know little or nothing about the person behind the legend.

At the pinnacle of the legends business, "heroes" are created every day. Reality shows have generated bountiful crops of new legends to admire. An individual may have been marginally featured in one reality show, then "fired" or voted out, only to become an instant legend. Today, it seems that every popular reality show participant reaches demigod status overnight and is soon invited to dispense advice, as if participating in one inane television production has bestowed some priceless knowledge on him or her. Arrogantly, these individuals publish books sharing their views on relationships, business, politics, and any other topic we are willing to let them pontificate on. We consume this material rabidly, even when the source is a 23-year-old whose only notable achievement in life has been getting "fired" by Donald Trump on TV.

We expose ourselves to this hazardous celebrity material not as a form of inspiration but as a shield. It becomes our excuse: The bar is too high; I will never make it, and it's too much trouble to try, so I might as well just buy the book (or the T-shirt or the perfume or the calendar or the posters—you get the point).

Reading about excellence is one thing we know how to do very well. Purchasing excellence is another way of avoiding the real thing. We will not do it, but we'll buy the souvenir. We'll leave excellence to others and buy the keepsakes while denying the truth. And the truth is this: The Excellence Myth fuels our imaginations in the wrong way; it does not inspire us to reach higher, it allows us to give up without even trying. Wonderful—we've outsourced excellence!

The Excellence Myth is perpetuated every time we admire one of our excellence icons. We treat these people with undue deference and often refer to them as legends, and a legend is what each amounts to—something from a fairy tale, not of the real world. Legends belong in storybooks, not in our lives. Our iconic legends are so far removed from our own situations that they no longer inspire us. The end result? We give up doing our best. When excellence is unattainable, we cannot be inspired. We will quit before we try.

The Culture of Dilbertism

The secret to success is knowing who to blame for your failures.

For every winner, there are dozens of losers. Odds are you are one of them.

It is always darkest just before it goes pitch black.

Dreams are like rainbows. Only idiots chase them.

Never underestimate the power of stupid people in large groups.

These quotes are from cards and posters produced and sold by Despair.com, a Web site and store dedicated to the "reality" of work.

Specializing in "Demotivators," Despair.com pokes fun at every conceivable endeavor and element of human motivation. Emblematic of its philosophy is the "Pessimist's Mug" that features a horizontal line across the middle and the words, "This glass is now half empty." Sure, I find some of this material very funny. I also find *Dilbert* funny. Scott Adams's cartoon offers an uncanny depiction of some companies where I once worked. I'm amazed by his ability to portray my ex-boss in such accurate detail. *Dilbert* and its copycats, from the BBC's (and now NBC's) TV show *The Office* to Despair.com products, deliver comic relief from corporate insanity. But is that all there is to it?

> Have you noticed that there are too many incompetent people in the world? Personally, I've been incompetent at virtually every job I've ever had. Yet somehow I always managed to get paid. Sometimes I even got awards. As far as I can tell, acting like you know what you're doing is just as profitable as knowing what you're doing and it's a lot less work. Attitude succeeds where experience and skill dare not venture.
>
> —Scott Adams

These words of *Dilbert* creator Scott Adams, from his book *You Don't Need Experience If You've Got Attitude*, say it all: If you can escape real work, do it. No one will notice and, besides, you are surrounded by incompetent people, so why try?

When your convictions are in such dire straits, "excellence" does not even enter the realm of possibility.

Over the years, the culture of Dilbertism has expanded widely. In some ways, we all have become Dilberts: cynicism experts inspired to spread the gospel. Much of it is shared via email, as Internet jokes. You know these messages well: They arrive with a long trail of people who've already read them. You'll often find just three lines of humor following 600 lines of forwarding addresses and "You GOTTA read this!!" Occasionally, there's a 5MB attachment with a full PowerPoint presentation, dedicated to corporate mediocrity. (I've often wondered who has the time to create these sizable presentations.) Many of these jokes and presentations are dedicated to the dysfunctional side of our working lives, the new heights of management stupidity, and the overall doomed state of the modern-day corporation.

If you love *Dilbert*, there's also the popular French book, *Bonjour Laziness*, by Corrine Meier, which has been translated into many languages including English. The book warns employees about the dangers of working hard, and for that matter, of working, period. The author depicts the moron boss and the stupid, unappreciative organization, and calls for all employees to fake performance and simply survive to collect a paycheck. She stresses that any other behavior is a waste of time and effort. The culture of Dilbertism is all around us, worldwide.

At this point, you may be wondering if I simply lack a sense of humor and if I can appreciate a good joke. After all, we've all been taught that whatever we can laugh at, we can overcome. We've been told that laughter is the best medicine, and that, with laughter, we can survive just about anything. Philosophically speaking, I believe laughter is an effective weapon that the weak can brandish against the strong, and that, all in all, humor is good for us. I have nothing against humor. In fact, some of my friends would argue that I tell a pretty good joke. Why, then, am I making an issue out of *Dilbert* and other cynical humor of this ilk?

The issue at hand is not humor per se. No doubt humor provides new perspective and helps get us through tough times. Humor plays an important role in human life and society. What I'm talking about here is not humor in general, but rather, consistently negative and debilitating humor. Humor that reinforces our weaknesses or inaptitude has a potentially damaging effect by helping to perpetuate the problem rather than inspiring us to achieve excellence. If our professional philosophy is merely to survive work and to get through it with the least amount of effort, we have no chance of reaching excellence because we are too busy surviving and accepting minimal performance as standard practice. My argument is only against humor that reinforces our powerlessness and reduces our capacity for excellence. The damage it causes is much greater than we imagine.

Before I continue, let me be emphatically clear about one thing: I place no blame on either *Dilbert* or its creator, Scott Adams. He is just the messenger. (Sure you can try to "kill" the messenger, but aren't we on the path away from quick fixes?) However, we should consider the message. These books, cartoons, and jokes are symptomatic of a growing culture of Dilbertism that raises serious questions for anyone who is personally committed to excellence or wants to be:

- If you work for a stupid company and a moron boss, what does that say about you?

- Why do you choose to subject yourself to this inaptitude?

- Are you willing to give up on your own potential?

- And, by the way, how is it that your company succeeds despite all the mediocrity surrounding you?

These questions manifest themselves in many ways, for both organizations and leaders alike. If you are a manager or executive, consider the following:

- If every cubical in your company is plastered with *Dilbert* cartoons that your employees find descriptive of the workplace, what does that say about you?

- What kind of people have you selected to be on your team, and what impact do they make on your performance?

- How competitive can your firm be when the level of employee confidence in the company is comparable to that of *Dilbert* characters?

- What level of performance can you expect from such a workforce?

- And, most importantly, how does the willingness of your people to perform impact your ability to achieve your financial objectives?

I have a confession to make. I was once addicted to *Dilbert*. (I am progressing in my 12-step *Dilbert* recovery program, though some symptoms persist.) Although I never engaged in pasting *Dilbert* strips all over my office, I did use them in presentations. In one case (which I can hardly believe now), I had a conference organizer pay for the rights to use a *Dilbert* cartoon about dysfunctional call centers. Whenever I presented the cartoon, I could count on chuckles from the audience. The crowd laughed and nodded their heads in agreement as if I had just described their CEO in excruciating detail.

Laughter is something every speaker strives for, but I soon realized that the laughs this cartoon strip garnered came at the expense of the audience's commitment to excellence. In readily accepting the *Dilbert* view of organizations, the individuals in my audience stripped themselves of responsibility and ownership. The more *Dilbert* they consumed, the less likely they were to take initiative, to work harder, to make new things happen, and, in general, to be held accountable for their performances. The message was all about inaptitude and the inability to change things in an environment of mediocrity. My audience believed in *Dilbert* and related to him. As a result, they believed in their own inaptitude.

The long-term price I was paying for my *Dilbert* addiction was way too high to merit the short-term chuckles I managed to squeeze out of my audience. By buying into the joke, they sold out their ability to change and make an impact. *Dilbert* debilitated them. *Dilbert* deteriorated their motivation and weakened their belief in their ability to create and deliver excellence. The addiction was taking its toll, and I had to stop cold turkey.

The culture of Dilbertism is nothing more than a quick fix. Like an addict, we cannot withdraw because we enjoy the temporary cynical joke. But as with any other fix, we ignore the long-term impacts, such as the gradual destruction of our commitment and belief in our capacity for excellence. The culture of Dilbertism inflates the Excellence Myth by reinforcing our perceived inability to achieve excellence.

Declaring war on *Dilbert*—by demanding, for starters, that all those cartoons be immediately removed from the office walls—will not solve the problem. In fact, it is more likely to accelerate it. While I would prefer not to see *Dilbert* dominating the office landscape, the cartoons should never be removed by order of the same executive they are intended to ridicule. The only way to eliminate them effectively is the natural way—by having employees recognize that you no longer act in the fashion shown in these cartoons. You can nurture an environment that will make *Dilbert* irrelevant by delivering excellence yourself, but you can't dictate it. We will discuss this further in the chapter dedicated to excellence management.

The Theory of Excellence

Our bookstores are overflowing with books about superior performance and excellence. We consume these books in tremendous numbers and make their authors rich and famous. These business heroes continue the journey through speaking engagements geared to tout their findings and presumably make us all more successful overnight. The question is, why has our overall performance not increased as a result of all this information? Considering the number of weeks *Good to Great* stayed on the *New York Times* bestseller list, we should have increased the annual GDP at least 2 points by now.

There are various types of books out there espousing excellence, of which I will mention the two most common. The first genre reflects the academic approach. The authors deconstruct, in ice-cold fashion, certain successful companies and then observe the "universal" rules of success. Unfortunately, readers of such books are often so overwhelmed by the magnitude of the ideas presented that they give up without even trying to implement them. These academic books, with their scientific approach, create excellence guidelines that are more retrospective of their research than they are useful tools for the reader. Ideas that work for a given company are often a reflection of that firm's DNA, history, and market conditions, and, thus, the results are unlikely to be replicated elsewhere. Some of these books suggest a leadership style, at whatever level, that is simply not applicable to other work environments. Recognizing this incongruity, the reader simply dismisses the ideas or principles.

In general, these academic books reinforce the Excellence Myth by painting a picture of excellence as heroic and difficult to achieve, and as the domain of senior management. Instead of inspiring organizations and individuals to abandon mediocre performance, they trap them there, feeling helpless and incapable of change.

The "I made it, you can make it, too" books belong to another genre that promises to increase your performance, but typically delivers just the opposite. Be it by a superstar CEO or an entrepreneur, most of us have probably read a book that explains how easy it is to make it happen right here right now. Reading these books reinforces the myth of easy overnight success. However, when we carefully examine the success stories, we become less energized as we recognize the discrepancies that make them less than relevant to us. When you read an "I made it" book, how often do you feel confident in your ability to deliver similar performance? Most readers gradually recognize subtle but important differences between their situation and the author's, as well as the unique opportunities the author enjoyed along the way. The amazing successes described in these books often seem so far beyond reach that readers will simply throw their hands up. Larger-than-life stories don't help most readers in the pursuit of excellence; they are more likely to dampen expectations, given the incompatible situations they present.

Neither the academic nor the "I made it" books help us dig out of the Excellence Myth, but rather keep us right in it. We come away more convinced than ever that we are small and incapable of greatness, with the attitude of inaptitude cemented in our minds more firmly than ever. Clearly, the desire and ability to deliver excellence isn't going to flourish if we don't believe we're capable of it in the first place.

Now What?

The Excellence Myth is nothing more than an illusion separating us from our own greatness. Even though we may not make the conscious choice to subscribe to this myth, it has the same serious impact, which is to prevent us from achieving excellence.

In reality and in contrast to the myth, excellence is all about maximizing *our* potential—being willing to do *our* best and then a bit more. Maximizing *our* opportunities where *we* live and work and under *our* conditions. The key word here is "our." Excellence is about each of us individually and the sum of our work as a group. Any time we are willing to make the effort to reach beyond our comfort zone, we are treading on excellence performance. When we feel the butterflies in our stomach, that's a sign we are reaching toward excellence. When we shift out of autopilot and strive at creative solutions aimed at helping someone rather than making excuses for why we shouldn't bother, we are in the territory of excellence.

There is no one standard of excellence, as the Excellence Myth would have us believe. A task that is impossibly difficult for one person will be easily mastered by another, but while not everyone is capable of climbing Mount Everest, each of us is capable of climbing to our own new heights. Each individual needs to find his or her personal standard of excellence and strive for that level of performance. What these individual excellence standards have in common is that they all push the individual to perform beyond what they think they can do. If you are confident in your ability to achieve your goal, you may be aiming too low; if you do not fear failure, then you are not striving for excellence.

Excellence Every Day?

Some people will view "excellence every day" as an oxymoron. We have been conditioned to think of excellence as something that occurs infrequently, as a once-in-a-lifetime performance that inspires us all and will not be repeated any time soon. We may define excellence as "overcoming huge challenges," or, in business, equate it with a decision that led to a major turn-around or a measure that resulted in landing a major customer account. These are definitely degrees of excellence, but it's a critical mistake to disregard our ability to deliver excellence in an everyday fashion. The fact is that daily excellence prepares us for the huge challenges life will present to us. Consider daily excellence as a form of training: the habit of excellence constantly evolving toward newer heights of performance.

Every day we face many moments of truth, daily choices that present opportunities for excellence performance. I refuse to accept the conviction that we are doomed to a life of mediocrity with an occasional cameo by excellence, appearances so rare that they become the rule. The rule should not be that excellence is rare. Every one of us is capable of delivering excellence every single day in every interaction, if we only choose to do so. We each have opportunities every day to extend excellence to friends, strangers, and customers alike. The answer to the question, "Is excellence achievable every day?" is an emphatic "Yes!" Excellence every day! It is a personal choice. Excellence is not determined from above: Don't blame God, your boss, or any other external factor for your inability to achieve an inspired performance and deliver exceptional results. We are all capable of delivering excellence, if we just stop believing that it is so difficult.

To dispel the Excellence Myth, we must start by redefining excellence. We need to stop defining it from the perspectives of others and start defining it from the viewpoint of our own capabilities. The timeframe of excellence needs to be adjusted as well. Rather than labeling it as a rare happening, excellence has to be defined as an everyday event. Every action has the distinct potential for excellence. By adjusting our definition of excellence to focus on our own capacity and framing its timing as "now and every day," we can start down the road to leaving the Excellence Myth behind and begin a journey of discovering our own capacity to deliver superior results and increase our competitiveness as individuals and as organizations.

In Chapter 3, we will look at how to create a definition of excellence that unleashes the potential within us. Before we approach the next chapter, though, you are invited to take a personal challenge. The *Excellence Aptitude Test* that follows will allow you to examine your personal perceptions of what excellence is, and to better understand how the Excellence Myth is affecting your ability to succeed.

The Excellence Aptitude Test

Rank each comment on a 1–5 scale where 1 = "Strongly Disagree" and 5 = "Strongly Agree"

- [ ] My workplace strategy is competitive and successful.
- [ ] My boss is a competent and respected leader.
- [ ] I work with people who support my pursuit of excellence.
- [ ] I live up to my excellence potential.
- [ ] I get many compliments for the quality of my work.
- [ ] I can see the results of my work.
- [ ] My work impacts others in a significant way.
- [ ] I am fully responsible for the results of my work.
- [ ] My work is personal and not just business.
- [ ] I have the tools and authority to do my job.
- [ ] In my organization, technology is secondary to people.
- [ ] I always strive to do more for customers.
- [ ] Decisions are not controlled by senior management.
- [ ] I always do what is right for the customer.
- [ ] My values and the organization's values are fully aligned.
- [ ] I am excited by the results of my work.
- [ ] Everyone can be as great as the top achievers of our century.
- [ ] I can recognize excellence in my daily work.
- [ ] Excellence is not a once-in-a-lifetime achievement.
- [ ] I will take risks to do the right thing.
- [ ] **TOTAL OF THE ABOVE**

SCORING:

20–49

You are a captive of the Excellence Myth. All the possible excuses for why you cannot deliver excellence are neatly arrayed in your *Dilbert* utility belt. You believe that your destiny, and therefore, your performance, is controlled by outside forces that you believe stop you from living up to your excellence potential. It might be short-term reassurance to think that others are stopping you from reaching your potential, but in the long term, it is your life and fulfillment we are talking about. Rethink your assumptions and find ways to live with the obstacles you believe exist in your life, while still striving for—and delivering—excellence.

50–79

You try to deliver excellence, but somehow fail to do so. The good news is that you see your potential. The bad news is that your excellence performance is misguided. You need to rethink your definition of excellence and re-evaluate the severity of some of the perceived obstacles. Carrying a project all the way through and not depending on others for the completion may help you see that you are personally capable of delivering excellence. Give yourself a chance and pursue it all the way to success.

80–100

You refuse to take no for an answer. Despite the challenges, you see the potential of your efforts and strive to perform in a superior manner. You do not allow challenges to stand in your way. You recognize them but still take responsibility to make a difference. You are proud of the impact you have on others and draw personal fulfillment and satisfaction from delivering excellence. You are on the right path. Continue to raise the bar and reach for new heights of excellence. Keep up the good work!

CHAPTER 3

Why We Fail to Delight Our Customers (While We Think We Do)

I have yet to come across a company or employee who does not declare total commitment to customers and excellence.

A commitment to performance excellence and to delivery of amazing customer experiences has been on the corporate agenda for years. I don't know about you, but I've heard it so many times that I've stopped counting. It is the most used and abused management mantra I know. Executives tout it to employees at every opportunity, establishing one initiative after another to support their commitment. Yet, for all the memos, T-shirts, campaigns, and programs, our customers are increasingly disappointed with the quality of service we deliver.

Three years ago, I set out to discover the root causes behind the failure—in spite of the best intentions of executives and employees—to satisfy our customers. I could not consolidate the lofty declarations of commitment with the lagging results in terms of loyalty. "Why can't we get it right?" was the nagging question in my mind. I was particularly intrigued by customer surveys and satisfaction reports. Companies aren't lacking for them. In fact, they have been accumulating vast collections of statistical analysis, pie charts, and graphs that apparently describe what the customer wants. The companies I investigated had a clear understanding that they were not living up to customer expectations, and yet no improvement was made following their analysis. They knew what was wrong, but failed to translate their insight into action.

My research, which would eventually extend to a survey of more than 23,000 individuals, sought to understand the reason for the gap between a firm's declared commitment to excellence and the reality. The research demonstrated that a root problem is the disconnect between employee and customer perceptions of what performance excellence is.

The employee attitude toward customer satisfaction studies boiled down to one thought: "It's all true, but it's not me—it's them." This suggests that many companies are losing the battle for excellence because employees fail to fully recognize their personal responsibility to, and the extent of their impact on, the customer experience. This was evident both in cases where employees directly interacted with customers (for instance, in sales and customer service functions) and where they impacted customers indirectly (for instance, in operational and legal functions). Interestingly, the vast majority of the employees described their performance as reaching a level of excellence. The anecdotal evidence showed that employees operate based on *their* definitions of excellence rather than the customer's, but research was clearly needed to prove it.

To identify the differences between employee and customer definitions of excellence, I designed the Experience Gap Analysis (EGA) study. The EGA study surveyed seven companies in the U.S. and Europe and allowed us to analyze 23,088 responses from 18,261 customers and 4,827 employees who served them. The survey asked both groups to rate the performance of the employees as they serviced the customers, with each group scoring the same performance event: the employees from their perspective as the deliverers of the performance and the customers from their perspective as the recipients. The customers and employees participating in the study represented a variety of sectors including business-to-business products, business services, and business-to-consumer products.

The EGA study presented the employees and their customers with an identical set of questions designed to explore prevailing definitions of "excellence performance" and to measure the customer experience on the following four dimensions:

1. Capabilities – The extent to which the employee possesses the necessary tools and authority to deliver excellence performance (e.g., access to customer information)

2. Knowledge – The extent to which the employee understands the customer's business, lifestyle, challenges, and aspirations

3. Willingness – The extent to which the employee is motivated to deliver excellence performance (e.g., to go above and beyond the call of duty)

4, Attitude – The extent and quality of the employee's connection with the customer (e.g., arrogance, sense of privilege to serve)

Each of these four dimensions was addressed through several questions relating to the way customers and employees interact and the outcome of that interaction. Questions were measured based on strong conviction responses rather than on median response.

The Gaps Tell the Story

EGA survey results revealed a significant disconnect between employee and customer perception, and nowhere was this more evident that in the "willingness" dimension with a 35.84 percent gap. Relative to customer responses overall, employees consistently overestimated their level of excellence performance, believing that they had delivered greater value than their counterparts on the receiving end were willing to give them credit for. A pattern in the responses showed that the criteria employees used in defining performance excellence generally neglected to take the customer's own criteria into account. Especially surprising were the following statistics:

- 79 percent of employees said they often go "above and beyond" and exceed customer expectations, yet only 29 percent of customers agreed. This is a 50 percent perception gap.

- 75 percent of employees said their work makes a difference in their customers' lives, but only 29 percent of customers agreed. This is a 46 percent perception gap.

- 88 percent of employees said they use common sense and discretion in the way they interact with customers, yet only 40 percent of customers agreed. This is a 48 percent perception gap.

These and other survey data established that employees' perceptions of their own performance often bear no resemblance to what the customer thinks. The results painted a picture of two distinct groups of interdependent people whose mutual expectations were not aligned. In general, based on the customer responses, employees were extremely unrealistic in their self-assessments.

In one international business-to-business company, the statement "I often go above and beyond" reached a perception gap of 66 percent. Some 90 percent of this firm's employees said they delivered above-and-beyond service, while only 24 percent of their customers agreed. This gap not only demonstrates a serious misunderstanding of customer expectations by employees, it highlights two incompatible realities. First, these employees applied one set of criteria to judge the quality of their service, and second, the customers rated the experience based on entirely different standards.

So, what is the reason for this employee confidence in the face of overwhelming customer dissatisfaction, as illustrated by the "willingness" gap? Is it arrogance? A 13 percent gap in the "attitude" dimension, which measures arrogance against humility, indicates that the problem has little to do with employee arrogance. In general, the customers did not perceive the employees as arrogant.

Another possible explanation for the gap was lack of tools and authority, assessed in the "capabilities" dimension. However, this dimension revealed the smallest gap of all, just 17 percent. Both customers (39 percent) and employees (56 percent) saw room for improvement when it comes to having the necessary tools, information, and authority to resolve problems right away. Thus, in the absence of a significant disagreement between employees and customers, the "capabilities" dimension did not allow us to explain the significant gap found in the "willingness" dimension.

We discovered the reason for the "willingness" gap when we evaluated the "knowledge" dimension data. The "knowledge" dimension—involving perceptions of how well employees understand their customers—yielded the second largest gap between customers and employees: 62 percent of employees said they understood the customers' business and related issues, while only 31 percent of customers agreed.

The following statistics from the "knowledge" dimension provide further insight into the basic lack of customer knowledge on the part of employees:

- 70 percent of employees said they understood customer pains and issues, but only 29 percent of customers agreed. This is a 42 percent perception gap.

- 84 percent of employees claimed to understand the value of their services to customers, but only 39 percent of customers agreed. This is a 45 percent perception gap.

- 56 percent of employees said they understood the business problem that it is their job to solve, but only 30 percent of customers agreed. This is a 26 percent perception gap.

Lack of employee knowledge of the customer's desired excellence performance was at the core of the failure to deliver excellence, not a lack of motivation. A further analysis of responses in the knowledge and willingness dimensions discovered a strong correlation between customers who claimed not to have received desirable resolution and those who claimed that employees did not understand their business, challenges, lifestyle, and aspirations. (These customers ranked employee performance significantly lower than those who said employees understood them.) Clearly, these employees did not have the full picture of where their products and services fit in the customers' lifestyles and what impact their performance had on customers. They failed to understand the hopes and aspirations of their customers, as well as the consequences to customers if their performance failed to deliver. By not fully understanding the impact of their actions, employees acted on their own preconceived—and often ill-conceived—notions of what the customer experiences "should have been." These results point to the fact that employees operate on a self-defined set of excellence criteria that have minimal overlap with the corresponding customer criteria.

This dissonance has little to do with employee attitudes or motivation levels and everything to do with the lack of clear definitions and insufficient knowledge of the customer. In the absence of clearly defined

excellence performance standards, employees default to their own definitions. Without understanding customers, employees are unable to
meet their expectations. "Excellence" is an abstract term and subject to
numerous interpretations. Only a mutually agreed upon definition of
excellence can lead to excellence performance.

"I Wish I Could Do More"

The EGA findings are not without a ray of hope. Even though the
surveyed employees were misaligned with their customers, they recognized the potential to deliver more than what they were delivering. Sixty
percent of employees agreed with the statement, "I wish I could do more
for the customer," and at one company, the number jumped to 82 percent. Good intentions, however, are rarely enough. Only 46 percent of
employees strongly agreed with the statement, "I have the tools and
authority to solve customer problems." These two statements highlight
what employees are really saying: Their ability to delight customers is
contingent upon their receiving the necessary tools, information, and
authority. Employees are indicating that they *want* to do more for customers, but they need their managers to provide better support.

Upon seeing the results of his organization's EGA, in which 92 percent of employees said they exceeded customer expectations compared
with only 26 percent of customers, one senior vice president remarked,
"This is embarrassing." However, such large gaps do not mean that
employees are unintelligent, incapable, or lazy. They are simply misdi-
rected, due to a lack of definitions and guidance. The large gaps point
to a self-centric rather than a customer-centric approach and to how
self-centric organizations fail to appreciate, build, and support processes
geared to delighting customers.

It is a total environment of excellence that is missing in today's
organization—a culture of excellence that begins with an ambitious

definition and follows through by emphasizing knowledge of the customer, providing empowering tools, and giving employees permission to execute. To achieve excellence, companies must make a leap. The EGA highlights the deep divide between self-centricity ("my" profits, "my" benefits) and customer-centricity, where it's always about exceeding the customer's expectations. Only by understanding what customers truly want and defining excellence from the customer perspective will organizations and their employees be able to deliver competitive performance excellence.

Excellence is in the eye of the beholder. The customer defines his view of excellence. Customers seek attention and want their needs, hopes, and aspirations to be taken into consideration. Above all, customers want someone who can deal with their problems effectively. Customers do not want half-baked efforts, and they despise being passed around the organization like a football. Declarations such as "we value the customer" and "customer service above all" ring hollow when executives fail to steer their employees toward customer experience excellence. True excellence must be defined and delivered with the recipient at the center of everything we do.

Simply starting by defining excellence from the customer perspective will let you leap forward. Working backward—starting with the desired customer outcome rather than by first attempting to change any internal process—will put you on the right track. In Chapter 4, we'll define excellence and begin our journey to living it every day.

Excellence—Defining, Believing, Living

Former British Prime Minister Margaret Thatcher once said, "Being powerful is like being a lady. If you have to tell people you are, you aren't." Thatcher's message is very clear: Certain things don't need to be publicized because your actions speak louder than words. If you do something truly great, there's no need to brag about it.

The same principle applies to excellence. If you deliver excellence, people are going to notice. (If they don't, it may not have been that great after all.) There will be no need to proclaim anything.

"Excellence is in the eye of the beholder" is a core principle that needs to be recognized in any definition of excellence. It is essential to the one we'll discuss here, relative to delivering superior performance to customers. The recipient of our performance determines its value, thus the way we define excellence hinges on his or her standards.

I find it amusing the way many companies advertise their commitment to excellence. Some use lofty slogans like "the relentless pursuit of perfection," while others tout their high customer-satisfaction rankings on billboards, in television ads, and through multimillion-dollar print and Web campaigns. Wouldn't you like to actually experience excellence rather than see it advertised to death? I know I would.

All this excellence advertising does not actually create any excellence. It doesn't even convince customers that these companies deliver excellence. Its only impact is to create higher expectations on the part of customers. The ads cue customers to expect more from these companies, putting you in deeper trouble: Your customer is now demanding more. Once the bar is raised, it is more difficult to deliver excellence and exceed expectations.

If you are truly committed to excellence, just do it.

But since we all strive for excellence, the big question remains: *What is excellence?* What does it look like? Can we actually define it? According to my dictionary, excellence is "the state, quality, or condition of excelling; superiority." I especially like the usage of the word "superiority," which clearly indicates that "consistency" and "parity" are not excellence. There is a higher level of performance that defines excellence.

I define excellence as the ability to exceed expectations. For me, excellence is simply the ability to surprise customers. It is the art of going beyond expectations, standards, and mandates, and beyond the expectations of your customers, your managers, and even yourself. When you go beyond expectations, you create something unique for your recipient. You add a personal touch and take responsibility. You contribute from the reservoir of your humanity. You surprise your customers (and sometimes yourself) with the creation of the new and impossible.

For a visual definition of excellence, just look in the eyes of a pleasantly surprised customer. She is lit up with appreciation and gratitude. You've made her day and brought a small ray of hope into her life. Remember that appreciative smile. That's the face of excellence as mirrored in the eyes of the recipient. This is what to look for when delivering excellence. When you see it, you'll know it.

Every recipient of the results of your actions is your customer. Excellence is not just the domain of those who serve external customers. Customers are everywhere, inside and outside your organization. A customer isn't just the person who physically purchases your products or services; he's anyone who must live with the consequences of your actions. If you're an IT professional, your customer is the employee who needs help when his computer crashes. As a worker in human resources, your customer is the new employee trying to navigate a new company culture. If you are the finance expert, your customer is that new manager who is having difficulty putting together her budget (or who has perhaps run out of budget altogether). For most of your actions there is a recipient, and that recipient is your customer. His smile of gratitude is your definition of the excellence you delivered.

As we discussed in Chapter 3, we need to redefine and reframe our conversation about excellence. It is a daily occurrence, something that we need to deliver on a regular basis, day in and day out. Everyone is capable of excellence, and every action is an opportunity for excellence. What makes a performance extraordinary is its impact on others, the ways in which it makes their lives better. People remember excellence. The greater the impact of a performance, the longer and more intensely it will be remembered, and, therefore, the higher the level of excellence attained.

Excellence starts with defining our objectives for going beyond, with setting the bar above expectations, and with targeting a surprised smile as the end result.

Excellence vs. Consistency

We often make the mistake of confusing excellence and consistency. Consistency is about optimizing services and products that are flawless.

By delivering a "consistent" product or service, we focus on removing elements of dissatisfaction and achieving parity.

At best, consistency meets customer expectations. Consistency is eliminating inaccurate invoices. Consistency is ensuring that all your products share the same level of quality. Consistency is responding to customer inquiries in a timely manner. It is heavily dependent on processes, and these processes become the primary objective of the performance; employees are merely executors of carefully managed procedures. In a consistency-driven environment, employees themselves are secondary to the process. They are subservient to the roles dictated to them by the process definition. Consistency emphasizes optimized processes and de-emphasizes the role of employees. At best, consistency reaches parity but never exceeds expectations.

Consistency is basically just doing your job. Some companies do it well; others do it in a mediocre way. Delivering consistency is nice, but it is not excellence—unless the rest of your industry is consistently awful and you stand out for being able to meet basic customer expectations. In fact, the definition of consistency is being on par with customer expectations. It is a boring, uninteresting place to settle. No one will celebrate your consistent performance.

Excellence and superiority, on the other hand, are about going above and beyond. They are about pleasantly surprising the customer. Excellence is all about exceeding expectations, not just meeting them. By definition, this type of performance requires human intervention to set higher goals, individualize and humanize the interaction, and be authentic throughout the entire experience. At the core of the contrast between consistency and excellence is the role of people and processes. With excellence, processes are merely tools that help people build a better solution. Employees are in charge, and it's up to them whether to use an established process. If it helps them achieve their goals, they use it. Otherwise, they use their discretion to get the job done and exceed expectations. With excellence, the corporate culture permits employee discretion and provides permission to perform, as well as permission to make mistakes.

Excellence requires an emotionally engaging performance that delivers an authentic and memorable caring touch. Processes cannot do this, only people can. So, excellence is not a matter of a better process. To achieve excellence, we need to place process in its rightful place, as a tool, and give people the freedom to perform.

Anticipating Needs

Unlike consistency, which is reactive in nature (you ask for something and the company delivers), excellence is all about being proactive, about anticipating the needs of the recipients of our excellence performance and delivering on them even before being asked. Your performance is characterized by generosity with a touch of surprise. You give your customer a little extra, surprising them with your thoughtfulness.

Generosity does not have to be characterized by losing money or giving away the shop. A bit of extra personal attention, a considerate comment, or a heartfelt expression of interest in the customer's well-being will do. Simply sending a birthday card can make a big impression. I'm amazed how few companies take the opportunity to make such simple gestures. In my experience, it is never a matter of cost but rather of mindset.

In a consistency world, we give customers what they have requested. In an excellence world, we shower them with more than they asked for to demonstrate our commitment to making a difference for them. In addition to anticipating customers' needs, we remember their preferences and are prepared to deliver on them the next time they call. This type of thoughtful preparedness lets customers know we're thinking of them even when they're not writing us a check.

One effective form of anticipating needs is to come up with a solution before the customer even knows there's a problem, which might include taking advantage of new technology. The history of business is full of examples of products and services we didn't know we needed—that is, until an excellence-loving company delivered them to us. The Sony Walkman was initially rejected by customer focus groups because participants could not envision walking in public with headphones on and music playing in their ears. But Sony decided to go ahead anyway, and, in 2004, on the 25th anniversary of the Walkman, the company shipped its 300 millionth unit. Not only was the product a commercial coup for Sony, but the impact of the company's bold ingenuity continues to be seen in the phenomenal success of Apple's iPod.

Some may argue that anticipating customer needs, showing generosity, and creating a sense of surprise are costly propositions. But consider the alternative: consistency. Consistency not only fails to build loyalty, it places your products and services at the level of commodities, which eventually leads to pricing pressure and discounting. On the other hand, customers will pay a premium for excellence, precisely because it has become such a rarity. When customers view your offerings as excellent and when you have earned their loyalty and repeat business through anticipating their needs, the cost of sales and marketing are reduced. Delighted by their experience, customers deliver an authentic, convincing message via word-of-mouth, which doesn't need a multimillion-dollar advertising budget to work. It is simply a trade-off between investing to deliver superior performance and value or investing to convince customers to come back to a mediocre experience.

Investing in excellence is an investment in building strong brand recognition and a customer commitment that leads to customer loyalty in repeat business and product or service evangelism. Financial considerations quickly fade as we come to appreciate the attention and excitement that excellence performance delivers.

Response–Ability

Responsibility is the opposite of process-following performance. Responsibility is focusing on our response to others. In responsibility, another person is on the receiving end and will be impacted by the outcome of our actions. In his book *Healing a Fractured World*, Rabbi Jonathan Sacks suggests that the word "responsibility" consists of the combination of *Response* and *Ability*. The ability to respond and to own the impact on the other person is at the heart of responsibility. Therefore, it is the essence of excellence. When we are held accountable for our actions, and when we view our performance through the lens of the outcome for others, the focus on our performance changes. There is no excellence without individual responsibility.

When you take responsibility, it's personal. The process becomes secondary when you're in charge. It's up to you to solve the problem, and it's your name on the dotted line. Responsibility is a matter of outcome. You might be able to perform all the necessary actions, but if the outcome is not satisfactory, your response has failed—a classic case of "the operation was a success, but the patient died." This kind of failure is very personal, and if you look at it honestly, you'll often find that failure is due to focusing on the process instead of taking ownership of the end goal.

Every task you face, every request you receive, every report you are asked to deliver, and every email that reaches your inbox needs to be viewed from a single perspective. Every action needs to be viewed not from the series of actions it requires to achieve completion, but from the impact it delivers to the recipients and, therefore, the complete scope of response it requires. This is responsibility: the complete ownership of the results.

If you're running a business, how do you develop a sense of ownership among your people? How can you ensure they take responsibility? While training employees to adhere to rigidly defined processes, many companies are achieving something entirely unintended: They are stripping responsibility for the outcome from their people. Employees receive the message that their job is not to think, but rather to follow rules. When the process was optimized, all the thinking was completed, and now it's time to perform the procedure.

This "don't-think-and-follow-the-rules" message is not the one most corporations intend to send to employees, but unfortunately, it is the outcome. As it's drummed into their consciousness, employees abandon common sense to follow the rules robotically. In so doing, they stop holding themselves accountable for the outcome.

When an employee follows the rules without taking ownership of the outcome (as often happens in a process-centric organization), he does not *care* about the outcome. This employee is simply completing tasks and is oblivious to the final result and impact of his work. The outcome is the result of the optimized process and belongs to the abstractness of the process, not to the employee. The employee's focus is on the specific action he or she is required to conduct. Like a worker on an assembly line, he is held accountable only for his specific component or action, not for the end result. The mindset becomes: The end result is someone else's problem so long as I get my job done. Welcome to the world of finger-pointing. You can always blame the process for the dissatisfaction of customers, or for a faulty product off the production line. In sticking to a predefined process and executing only a fraction of the complete product's manufacture, you are absolved of responsibility.

To achieve excellence, order must be brought to its natural state. Employees need to be placed in the pilot's seat and processes must be regarded as tools to achieve a goal. Managers must permit employees to take charge. They have to recognize and support this shift in priorities and provide an excellence-enabling environment. Without the ability to respond, which means full understanding of the recipient and the power to lead the process and not be led by it, excellence cannot be delivered.

For their part, employees need to reawaken their willingness to accept responsibility and take ownership of the outcomes of their work. Hiding behind processes will not lead anyone to excellence; recognizing the existence of the recipient and focusing on "response-ability" will. The combination of focusing on the recipient and of understanding his or her needs, while taking full responsibility for the outcome of the performance, produces the winning combination of factors that create excellence. This two-part approach can be used effectively by anyone seeking to push his performance into the excellence domain.

The Art of the Human Touch

What is the cost of a sincere smile? I remember once entering a hotel very late at night. The desk clerk was so detached and robotic in his actions that I offered him a dollar for a really good smile. All I wanted was a smile. For those of you who are curious, the employee finally got the message, and I got my smile (and got to keep my dollar as well).

It doesn't cost anything to provide a human touch, yet it is such a powerful action.

A human touch can come in different forms, from a warm smile to simply addressing the customer by name or from inquiring about the customer's trip to acknowledging jet leg or stress that he may be feeling. It's any person-to-person gesture that represents a human connection. It's any method that involves personalizing your actions to make a customer feel at home, to feel cared for and welcome. Anytime a customer feels she is being helped by a real person and not by a machine, a human touch has been delivered.

In any situation where a customer is being served, human touch is a critical dimension of excellence. A genuine caring that touches people in a meaningful way has a powerful effect on their perception of any experience. Excellence has less to do with big investments and major strategic initiatives and more to do with an attitude, one that reflects a personal commitment to serve and delight customers. We should view the opportunity to be of service as a privilege. Helping others is a wonderful and satisfying experience, and when we tap into this attitude and commitment, it allows us to deliver a human touch and connect with our customer on a personal level.

In reflecting on your youthful dreams and aspirations, you may recall wanting to make a difference in people's lives. Once you begin to view your everyday performance from the perspective of the recipients of your actions, I think you'll find you have not moved that far from those early aspirations; you will recognize that your most idealistic goals are still valid, and you will find that you are closer to actualizing your excellence than you realized.

On a recent trip overseas, I counted 13 airline employees and immigration officers who opened my passport and examined my personal information. It was my birthday, yet not one of them wished me a happy birthday. A gesture like that would not have cost anything. It would not have required approval from the CEO. It would have simply required attention by the individual. Service to customers should be nothing like handling transactions; rather, it involves the recognition that the voices and faces you encounter belong to living, breathing human beings. Sadly, most employees focus on completing the task at hand, treating the individual involved as if he was invisible. They perform in a robotic manner, not connecting with their own humanness.

Companies that fail in their pursuit of excellence are typically geared to meeting ever-rising quarterly sales quotas, viewing their customers as a series of transactions. They fail to see the person behind the transaction and, thus, they miss the opportunity to connect and create excellence. If they only realized that there is an upper limit to how many customers can be gained through transaction efficiency but virtually no limit to the number of customers who can be gained through compassionate service, these companies would be making very different choices than those they make today.

A human touch in the overall experience can be the critical factor in a firm's success, but under one condition: If the products or services do not meet customer expectations, no human touch will be able to erase the deficiency. It is only on the basis of good products and services, led by a human touch, that we can build emotionally engaging experiences. You can do it, but only if you *want* to do it.

Early in the Morning

When I boarded a small 40-seater airplane for a 6 A.M. flight from Louisville to New York, I was still half-asleep. To make the flight, I had to get up at 4 A.M. To my surprise, the flight attendant, Diane, was in a cheerful mood and greeted me with a great smile and welcome. My response was, "I can't believe you can be so cheerful at this hour." Apparently, Diane understands how difficult it is for anyone to wake up before dawn to make an early flight because she made an effort—a genuine effort—to make us all comfortable. When she made the preflight instructional announcement, she used her own words rather than the scripted text, and even her announcement about not smoking incorporated a sense of humor. While serving refreshments, she made a point of chatting with the young mother traveling with a 15-month-old baby. She took the time to talk with the passenger in 15A about the book he was reading, and made an all-out effort to make everyone feel as relaxed as possible.

As the New York skyline appeared, Diane became our tour guide, pointing out different sites we could see while flying over Manhattan. She was authentic in her caring. She did not relate to her work as a job but as a mission. That is how she delivered excellence and not just consistency.

It is the small touches that make a difference. It is about bringing out the best in yourself and sharing it with others. As with Diane's smile, the more you share, the more you have. It doesn't cost you anything to smile sincerely, and it may actually create a chain reaction.

Excellence is often as simple as ABC:

- Anticipate needs

- Be generous

- Care

Smiling sincerely is a form of generosity. Being willing to share your thoughts and attention with others is another form of generosity, the "generosity of human touch." This is the type of generosity that no one can buy; it depends on the giver. As a frequent business traveler, I have always believed that airlines are really in the business of caring, of helping passengers feel at home while traveling. To my disappointment, most airlines do not understand or strive to deliver this kind of service. Too many view their business as a series of take-offs and landings, made profitable through the fuel-efficient management of the process.

Diane didn't need her CEO to tell her how to deliver excellence. She didn't need a 10-inch-thick manual that emphasized the importance of caring and explained how to act like a human being. She knew from her own experience that predawn flights are hard on passengers, and she tapped into her personal resources to deliver a beyond-expectation performance then and there.

Sincerely Yours

Although excellence can be difficult to define, as recipients, we know it when we see it. We can tell when someone is going the extra mile, and we appreciate and remember these experiences. For those who go above and beyond, we will go above and beyond in return. The good-will earned by companies that inspire and nurture excellence within their ranks is impossible to overestimate.

Reaching beyond what's acceptable, taking responsibility for the results, being authentic and caring, and providing surprising and delight-ful outcomes are all critical dimensions of excellence for the customer-focused firm. As organizations and as individuals, we need to define excellence as a quality that far surpasses mere consistency. Keeping up with competitors isn't enough anymore. We need to deliver unique and memorable experiences that reflect our unique excellence capacity.

Excellence is not process-driven but, rather, it's *impact*-driven. It is not the sum of all the mechanical tasks we complete satisfactorily. It does not result from well-written manuals or enlightened mission statements, but from the way we conduct our business.

The ultimate definition of excellence is in the eye of the beholder, and when you see a customer's surprise in response to an excellence perfor-mance you delivered, you know you have achieved it. Excellence is defined by the things *you* do, not by what other people do. Excellence is defined by what you do today—*now*—not what you might do in the future.

Excellence is not about heroes; it's about you. It is about what you choose to do today with the opportunities presented to you. It is a mat-ter of personal choice—your Daily Choice for excellence.

From defining excellence, we move to delivering it. Our Daily Choices are the means by which we can deliver excellence and maximize our performance capacity. What are these choices and how do we make them happen? The answers are just ahead.

The Daily Choice You Make—Delivering Excellence One Decision at a Time

You are on the phone with an upset customer. Your company disappointed her, treating her unfairly in her eyes. You listen empathetically and nod your head in agreement (can she actually see you nodding your head?). It *was* unfair treatment, in your opinion—no one should be treated that way. You know how it feels. You've been on the other side many times, and if you were in her shoes, you would be reacting the same way. Deep down, you know she is right and deserves to be treated better. But ... (and there is always a "but").

But you are not authorized to do what you think is right for the customer. You know what you believe should be done, but it is either out of your control or will require a major effort to get it approved. According to the company manual, you are supposed to use a scripted message that refuses to accept responsibility and fails to provide a meaningful solution. But sometimes the rules and procedures are inadequate or unclear, or there are no predefined guidelines even remotely appropriate to the situation. Now what? What are you supposed to do?

This is a moment of truth. From the customer's perspective, you don't have too much time to respond. She's extremely upset, and an indifferent response or useless excuse will only make matters worse. For her, it is *the* moment of truth—the only moment that she's willing to grant you.

This moment of truth is a prime example of how and when to use your Daily Choice. You can either stick to the rules, despite the fact that they are woefully inadequate, or you can do what you know is right for the customer. This is the choice between consistency and excellence. It is the choice between hiding behind illogical excuses or delivering high-impact performance that will make a difference.

In every interaction that we have with people, be it our fellow employees or our customers, the Daily Choice confronts us. What will you do? Succumb to the manual or re-create the rules? Act like a robot or choose to make a difference and treat others the way you would want to be treated? Take responsibility or blame someone else?

You can always blame the "system" because every company has a system to hide behind. But will you be able to sleep at night after playing the blame game?

The Daily Choice is the essence of excellence. Making the right choice will enhance your capacity for excellence and strengthen your overall excellence performance. The choice to stick to the manual and hide behind corporate excuses will weaken your excellence position.

When you make the choice for excellence, you have chosen to be a subject rather than an object. You have chosen not to be helpless but rather to wield your power to make things happen. As an object, you are told what to do, and you are expected to blindly follow the rules. As a subject, you use your heart, intelligence, and any and all available resources to do what needs to be done.

We all need to ask ourselves whether we are making the Daily Choice for excellence. Consider the following examples:

- What will you do with the 20 to 50 emails you receive today? Will you transfer the responsibility (or perhaps the blame), ignore them completely, or take ownership and handle each and every situation to the best of your ability?

- As a researcher with a challenging assignment, do you keep searching for the answer until you find it, or do you give up after becoming frustrated?

- As an IT professional, do you do whatever you can to solve the employee's computer problem, or spit out a scripted answer and blame the user for mishandling his machine?

- As a receptionist, do you make visitors feel welcome or treat them disinterestedly?

- In meetings, do you try to contribute or simply nod in agreement to suggestions that you do not agree with and have no intention of executing?

- As an HR specialist, do you look for ways to help an employee who is in personal financial trouble or act dismissively because, after all, it is not the company's responsibility?

- As a salesperson, do you try to identify the ideal solution to the customer's problem or push a product you know will not meet his expectations?

- As an insurance agent, do you try to expedite the claim of a customer in distress or relegate it to its "proper" place at the end of the queue?

Each of us faces a Daily Choice. We reach a juncture, every day, in each interaction, where we can turn to the left and simply follow the rules, making the minimum acceptable effort, or turn to the right and deliver excellence. If we choose the former, we may effectively move the problem off our desk, but we can be sure we are not going to delight the customer. The choice is between being indifferent and making a difference.

The funny thing about mediocrity is that, unlike excellence, you do not need to choose it. All you need to do is ignore an opportunity to perform with excellence, and your choice is made for you. Mediocrity happens when we do not pursue excellence; it does not have to be a conscious choice, it is the default choice. By not choosing excellence, you automatically make the choice *against* it. If your response to the customer on the phone is an illogical citation of a dated rule that does not apply to her case, you have made a choice against excellence. You have taken one more step on the journey to mediocrity and moved one step away from the path of excellence.

Choices or Chores?

As a manager, the concept of employees having a choice can be frightening. In many cases, it implies some loss of control. The recognition that employees determine the future of your organization through their actions represents a reversal of traditional roles. You may see employee choice as a recipe for chaos, but the reality is that it often occurs anyway—with or without your consent. The sooner you accept, embrace, and foster employee choice as a positive contributor to your organization's performance, the sooner you will begin delivering excellence every day.

Employees often regard top-down, mandated tasks as chores. Such tasks are not their chosen work; they don't like doing them, and many times, they don't see the point. It's only human to resent "don't-ask-questions-just-do-it" assignments. Reluctance is understandable. In the absence of any freedom of choice, these types of jobs are completed half-heartedly, not with enthusiasm and commitment. The result will be the opposite of excellence.

When you or any one of your employees makes a Daily Choice to perform a task, it comes with a full commitment. It is a choice as opposed to a chore. The decision is made with enthusiasm because you are fully committed to your choice. You want to make your choice a success. It is personal, not just business. You have a vested interest in the outcome when it's your choice rather than a command from the top. Introducing choice to employees raises both the level of commitment to performance and the level of performance quality within an organization.

Am I saying that every assignment requires the blessing and approval of employees? Of course not. However, every job you assign should come with the answer to the question, "Why?" Most managers forget to address this, and, without seeing the full picture and without understanding the purpose of an action, employees will not choose to do it and instead will view it as a chore. Building a process of open dialogue as opposed to a top-down command will go a long way toward enabling your employees to choose and, as a result, not to treat tasks as chores.

When fully understood and managed correctly, the employee's Daily Choice is not a threat but rather a promise to you—a promise to deliver excellence. This promise includes personal commitment and enthusiasm, and eliminates reluctance and half-hearted performance. Consistency may be achieved with reluctance, performed as a chore. Excellence requires the personal commitment that can only come with a choice made by your employees.

Does It Have to Be Every Day?

"Does it have to be choice all day, every day?" you ask. It can be tiring to make choices all the time, sometimes very hard ones, and simply following procedures can make life easy. Well, if you are willing to give up your humanity and growth for a while, go ahead and take a break from choice. Not making choices comes with a price, and there is no state of non-choice. Every time you fail to make a choice, you default to a choice in the opposite direction, a choice against achieving excellence today, a choice not to take responsibility, not to care, and not to make an impact. That's the choice to go through the motions rather than deliver superior performance.

"How do I make the right choice every time?" you ask. Consult your common sense. If you are focused on doing the right thing for others, whether they are customers or colleagues, you will make the right choice. If your focus is to treat others as you wish to be treated, then you will make the choice for excellence. If you take responsibility and care for others in the process, you will make the right choice. If you focus on the impact on others and not on the mechanical aspects of the task, you will make the right choice. If you follow your passion and not a predetermined list of actions, you will make the choice for excellence performance with impact.

Twenty Years to Overnight Success

When discussing success with people who have major achievements to their credit, you will notice an interesting pattern: While many will point to a breakthrough moment or event, they will also mention the many daily choices they made. Some will even cite poor choices they made.

An Olympic athlete has to resist many temptations in order to focus on his desire to perfect a performance and to win. Every day, the athlete has to choose between fun and entertainment (including mind-numbing activities) and being disciplined and focused on his goals. The level of excellence achieved, winning the gold medal or not, has more to do with the Daily Choices the athlete makes than with that one great opportunity.

All his many choices for excellence were building a discipline for excellence. Like building blocks, each Daily Choice you make will strengthen your capacity for excellence and raise the bar for what you can achieve. One day, you will discover that the Daily Choice has become second nature to you. You'll wonder how you could ever have considered delivering anything other than excellence.

This is the pattern of excellence through Daily Choices. We can sit and wait for the one big break, or we can start making it happen today. We can complain about our lack of luck in achieving a breakthrough, or we can create our own luck. Making the Daily Choice is the equivalent of training for excellence. It is training in real life, where your trials and errors actually have an impact on others. The more Daily Choices you make toward excellence, the more excellence performance you deliver and the stronger your faculty for excellence.

If you are waiting for your excellence to arrive in the form of overnight success, think again. Overnight success, like overnight excellence, requires discipline and training. The more excellence you deliver through Daily Choices, the stronger your capacity for success and the closer you'll be to becoming that overnight success.

Excellence Starts with You

Our deepest fear is not that we are inadequate; our deepest fear is that we are powerful beyond measure. It is our light, not our darkness that most frightens us. We ask ourselves, who am I to be brilliant, gorgeous, talented and fabulous? Actually, who are you not to be? You are a child of god. Your playing small doesn't serve the world. There's nothing enlightened about shrinking so that other people won't feel insecure around you. We were born to make manifest the glory of god that is within us.

> It's not just in some of us, it's in everyone. And as we let
> our own light shine we unconsciously give other people per-
> mission to do the same. As we are liberated from our own
> fears, our presence automatically liberates others.
> —Nelson Mandela, from his 1994 Inauguration Address

I could not articulate my point better than by quoting these words from Nelson Mandela. Excellence starts with you—yes, you. Not with your boss or your CEO. Not with basketball stars, politicians, Olympic winners, Hollywood actors, firefighters, or any other category of "hero." It starts with you. You are the boss of excellence, your own excellence. You are the decision maker when it comes to excellence performance in the daily opportunities you face. No one can make those decisions for you. As an individual, you are gifted with unique skills and capabilities. No one is more qualified than you to master the challenges that come your way. Your unique set of competencies and skills will allow you to embrace and take advantage of the opportunities presented to you, in your own way, as only you can do.

It is easy to fall prey to the consistency performance trap, where all your actions are predetermined by a job description, and you just follow the rules blindly. With consistency performance, your actions are mea- sured, predictable, and easy to duplicate. If you succumb to it, you will become interchangeable, replaceable, and subservient to the process. You will become a mere executor of a procedure that may soon be auto- mated altogether. A consistency performance is not the greatest moment in anyone's life and career. It does not allow for improvisation, caring, and individualizing actions for the benefit of the recipient. All that con- sistency performance does is strip you of your unique capacity for excel- lence, and therefore, your competitiveness. It makes you dispensable.

In excellence performance, on the other hand, you, not the process, are the primary driver. The procedures are merely tools of your trade, and if they do not fit, you have room to improvise and adapt to deliver excellence. The individual makes the performance. You determine the results. The results are different because they are personal to the recipient. Excellence performance renders you indispensable.

Excellence starts with small actions, so long as you are focused on the recipient and not on yourself. Imagine yourself at a party. All the guests are drinking and laughing and apparently having a great time. The only problem is that you don't know anyone there. Since you arrived, you've had a few drinks, snacked on some almonds, and pretty much become an inconspicuous component of the wallpaper. You lean on the wall, away from the party's center of gravity, scouting the scene and feeling lonely and sorry for yourself. Suddenly, your view is interrupted by a big, sincere smile and an introduction: "Hi, I'm David." He exudes friendliness. The conversation starts rolling, and all of a sudden, you're not alone anymore. One smile in a sea of strangers was all it took.

We have all been at parties and gatherings where our biggest claim to fame was becoming a semipermanent fixture. Each of us has been there, embarrassed and reluctant to start up a conversation with people we don't know. Now think about the previous story. What a great turn of events—David literally saved you from this party that seemed to be doomed. He made a choice to deliver excellence. No one sent him over to talk to you; he simply recognized the situation and did something about it.

As the recipient of this type of good deed, you can fully appreciate the action, the value, and how it made you feel. I have observed to flight attendants that they are actually in the loneliness business: I can get peanuts and water on any flight (well, given the current cost-cutting obsession, on almost any flight), but there are few airlines that provide sincerity and caring when I am traveling all by myself on business. A simple but sincere human touch can make all the difference in these situations. In a world of strangers, caring simply brightens your day with a warm touch.

I will never forget Claudia, a Lufthansa flight attendant who covered me with a blanket while I was sleeping on board. This was not in her job description. No one told her to do it. She made a choice, and with a simple act, she raised her actions from the level of mechanical consistency to one of overt humanity. Claudia could easily have ignored me, but she looked out for excellence opportunities and made a difference. Humanity *is* excellence. Our willingness to lend our humanity to others brings us to the pinnacle of excellence.

The Puzzling Paper Clips

When we conduct executive training, we like to play the following game. We give every executive a bunch of paper clips and a couple of pieces of a jigsaw puzzle. They are asked to pile these items together. Naturally, the paper clips are placed in one pile, while the puzzle is automatically put together. We ask the participants to estimate the number of paper clips. They never bother to count them, but instead provide a rough estimate. When we take some paper clips away, they hardly notice the difference. When they put together the puzzle, they notice one piece is missing. We try to convince them to frame the puzzle and place it on the wall for display; after all, one missing piece can't matter that much. They refuse, claiming that the puzzle is not complete without the missing piece. Then, we propose to replace the missing piece with another piece that is identical to *another* piece in the puzzle. That doesn't work either because in a jigsaw puzzle, one piece cannot take the place of another. Each piece is unique and necessary to complete the puzzle.

The point we are making to these executives is that their people often feel like replaceable paper clips and not like unique pieces of a larger puzzle. When the message they hear is about replaceable, interchangeable paper clips, they act and perform with little excellence involved. They go through the mechanical motions of completing the task, but no excellence is delivered. We need to transform perceptions so that our people realize they are critical to the organization, that the contribution of each is unique and important to the whole. Without the unique, irreplaceable excellence performance of each individual, the organization will not be complete. It is only when employees adopt this "I am important" state of mind, which requires managers and executives to change their attitudes and work styles, that the company can unleash excellence. It takes two to break a bad perception. As a worker, you can't simply wait for those at the top to make you feel valuable and capable of excellence— you need to get it started from within you. Remember that it only takes one smile in a sea of indifference to get it started.

Will Daily Choices solve the problem of world hunger? Perhaps not, but they will solve *someone's* hunger. While reading Rabbi Jonathan Sacks's *Healing a Fractured World*, I came across a story he quoted on behalf of the American anthropologist Loren Eiseley. An old man was walking on the beach at dawn when he noticed a young man picking up starfish stranded by the retreating tide and throwing them back in the sea one by one. He went up to him and asked him why he was doing this. The young man replied that the starfish would die if left exposed to the morning sun. "But the beach goes on for miles, and there are thousands of starfish. You will not be able to save them all. How can your effort make a difference?" The young man looked at the starfish in his hand and then threw it to safety in the waves. "To this one," he said, "it makes a difference."

Whether you are a 30-year veteran CEO or a 21-year-old employee starting your first job, you will always face Daily Choices. Despite the obvious differences in the decisions required of you as the CEO or the mail clerk, you face the same challenge. Will you choose to deliver impact through excellence, or will you default to mediocrity? Regardless of your role in the organization, your seniority, or the number of brilliant ideas you have brought to fruition in the past, you face new Daily Choices for excellence today. Every decision you make will have consequences that a customer will feel. You may choose to deliver excellence and delight the recipient, or deliver mediocrity and let him down. On this day, you are only as good as the choices you make toward excellence and away from mediocrity.

Managers have a dual Daily Choice: As individuals, you share the same Daily Choices as your employees; but as managers, you have a Daily Choice in how to manage your employees. You may choose to enable excellence or default to controlling processes. You may choose to accept mistakes while providing permission to perform, or you can keep employees on a tight lead, demanding blind obedience and suppressing initiative. The choice is yours. And there will always be a recipient at the other end of your choice.

This is the essence of the Daily Choice. Make a difference to this one customer or this one employee. In taking an action that makes such a difference you are putting yourself on the path to excellence. Make just one choice at a time, and you will see your excellence capacity become richer and stronger over time. And remember: No one can make the choice for you. You cannot follow the manual and call it a personal choice. Excellence is all about *you* making the choice *every* day.

As we've already discussed, process cannot be the ultimate goal. Processes should be employed as tools. If they fit the challenge, employees should follow them and then add a human touch to complete the excellence. However, there will be many times when a problem will require an outside-the-box solution. In these cases, employees should be permitted to make a Daily Choice to deliver excellence and to delight customers based on their special needs.

There is no doubt that because excellence is a matter of personal choice, managing it is tricky. You can't order your employees to choose excellence. They need to want to do it. You may demand, threaten, plead, or beg, but ultimately, it will be *their* choice. This choice by employees to deliver excellence is a shift in power that presents a serious challenge to managers everywhere: How can we manage our employees' choice to deliver excellence using the old tools of management? It seems as though the stick of top-down command and the carrot of salary does not apply here. Excellence is our gateway to competitiveness and innovation. We need every ounce of competitiveness and innovation we can get. So, the case for changing the way we interact, manage, and lead our people to obtain their commitment to excellence is stronger and more compelling than ever before.

How do you encourage people to make the Daily Choice to deliver excellence without a carrot or a stick? This question is at the heart of Chapter 6, which deals with managing challenges in an environment where traditional management tools have become irrelevant. Look at it as an invitation to redefine management and your role as a manager.

CHAPTER 6

Creating Organizational Excellence

Millions of Daily Choices Every Day

The average call center employee handles 40 calls each day and 10,000 calls every year. These calls represent some of the thousands of Daily Choices this employee has the opportunity to make every year. Top-down decisions from the CEO have little, if any, impact on this employee's Daily Choices.

For the average call center with 20 employees, there will be at least 2 million Daily Choices for excellence every year—2 million choices that will make the difference between excellence and mediocrity. If 2 million decisions are made at the call center for excellence, the company's performance and reputation will be strengthened; if they are made for mediocrity, the company will be diminished. The total value of the company is equal to the total of all the Daily Choices made by all its employees.

Using an example in another setting, the results are the same. A bank teller may handle an average of 30 customers a day, which alone accounts for 6,500 Daily Choices that he will make each year. If we assume that there are 10 employees per branch and 1,000 branches per bank, this amounts to at least 65 million Daily Choices a year. No advertising or branding campaign will be able to alter the results of these choices; they will cause the bank to be perceived as excellent, mediocre, or worse. The strength of the bank and its customer relationships does not lie in the competitiveness of its interest rates but in the performance choices its employees make every day.

A desk clerk at a 500-room hotel will check in and check out an average of 100 guests per day. These guests represent 100 Daily Choices that this employee will make during the course of just one shift. In a year, that's 25,000 choices for this one clerk alone. The loyalty that guests feel toward the hotel will be directly related to these choices, more so than to the images and offers created by the marketing experts. No marketing effort can overcome the poor choices made by frontline employees, and no advertising campaign can have a stronger positive impact on business than the Daily Choice for excellence.

Daily Choices take place in front of external and internal customers every day. They are dominant in interactions with other people, including staff meetings, email exchanges, phone conversations, and any situation where an individual is in a position to help someone else. Any time there is a recipient on the other end of the action, there's a Daily Choice involved.

The real power of organizations is their ability to create excellence, to differentiate themselves and, as a result, to build strong customer loyalty, earn repeat business, and charge a premium for their goods and services. This power (or lack of it) is directly linked to the quality of millions of Daily Choices made by employees. The bottom line is that a company's overall excellence is equal to the sum of the total excellence-seeking Daily Choices delivered by its people. There is no better way to measure the strength of a company than by the quality of the choices its employees make every day. The more excellence delivered, the stronger the customer's commitment and the greater the amount of business and profits generated. The weaker its employees' commitment to excellence, the weaker its overall performance. This is a new way to view the power and strength of organizations, and it requires a different way of leading and motivating people to generate Daily Choices for excellence and exceeding customer expectations.

This bottom-up organizational definition runs contrary to the way most organizations define themselves today. A top-down organization views its power, strength, and brand as an abstract entity, loosely connected to its people. The employees are subservient to the larger organizational definition. According to this line of thinking, even if all the employees leave the organization, the brand will remain strong; the brand makes the people and not the other way around. In a bottom-up organization, the organization is defined by the character and performance of its employees. The people in the company make the organization what it is. They are the ones creating the assets of the organization. Although some management and marketing theories value an organization based on its brand strength and reputation, these types of assets are actually wholly dependent on employees and their choices for excellence. Missing one excellence-oriented employee will make the company weaker. Poor performance by just one employee will make the company weaker. The company does not exist without the people who, through their Daily Choices, breathe life into the company's mission statement, values, objectives, strategy, and overall definition.

One employee at a time, one Daily Choice at a time, a company's strength is actually created. This company's definition is not an event or a milestone that, once achieved, always remains valid. Rather, it is an ongoing process that can reach new heights (or lows) depending on the Daily Choices made by employees. The company's success is not measured by some annual study of corporate brand strength, but by the daily performances of the individuals who *are* the company. Most companies declare their total commitment to their employees and tout their initiatives to promote employee welfare on the pages of their glossy annual report, while relatively few companies truly understand what it means to treat employees as their most important asset.

"You Must Smile Sincerely at All Times"

Every company can find among its ranks an isolated hero who consistently goes above and beyond. Many would argue that such performers will always remain the exception to the rule. But can we, in fact, institutionalize the above and beyond mindset?

In traditional management thinking, the answer is clear: You cannot mandate excellence. Consistency and process efficiency are the best you can hope for. Businesses that ascribe to this philosophy are not equipped to create and nurture a culture of excellence. Their management model is designed around compliance, and it comes at the expense of freedom to perform.

You cannot order people to care; they need to want to do so. Any attempt to force people to smile sincerely will lead to artificial gestures that customers will almost certainly recognize.

Once committed to building a culture of excellence, most of today's managers and organizations find themselves in uncharted territory. First and foremost, they are no longer in control, in the sense that they cannot dictate the desired result. Next, they need to implement new tools to achieve their goals. In essence, they need to study and practice the art of persuasion. They need to inspire excellence by creating an environment in which employees: (1) are allowed to perform, and even to fail; (2) are encouraged to go above and beyond; and (3) are rewarded for excellent results. Sincere smiles will come naturally when managers and executives commit to creating such an environment.

Firms are facing a serious challenge to their competitiveness because the old tools of the trade are no longer good enough. In fact, many of the tools that worked for top-down, military-style management models have become completely irrelevant, and today they are as outmoded as stone knives and bearskins. Traditional management tools were designed to manage consistency, processes, and output—not humanity and excellence.

"But what about the paycheck?" executives ask. "We pay them to perform." Well, today's paycheck buys you employee time and availability, but it won't buy you excellence. In other words, a paycheck may buy you consistent performance, but it won't guarantee excellence performance. For their salaries, modern employees can be expected to deliver on the mechanical requirements, but they may leave their hearts at home.

A paycheck may encourage employees to do the following consistently:

- Occupy their chairs

- Answer the phone

- Fill out forms

- Read and answer email

- Attend meetings

- Talk to customers

- Complete expense reports

- Take vacations

- Read memos

- Read the manual

- Adhere to safety rules

- Listen to the CEO

- Show up on time

- Visit the intranet

- Attend the annual holiday party

These requisite activities aside, the paycheck does not buy excellence. Excellence is directly linked to responsibility and accountability, and it is a voluntary act. If employees wish to pursue excellence, they will; and if they do not, you will never see a shred of it.

Studies have shown that only about 30 percent of employees find a sufficient level of personal satisfaction and fulfillment on the job to lead them to make a strong commitment to excellence performance. The vast majority of employees are categorized as either "neutral" or "negative" in their attitude toward their workplace. They come to work because they need the money, not because it challenges or fulfills them.

This is a tough reality check for many executives who would like to believe that they control their employees by paying their salaries. These executives are under the illusion that, at their whim, employees will do whatever is asked. The reality is quite different. In fact, the paycheck buys an organization the total of eight hours a day, plus the driving time to and from the office. Everything else is optional and subject to employee choice.

Just as managers cannot order people to be creative and come up with 35 innovative ideas per year, likewise they cannot mandate excellence. Creativity and innovation, as with excellence, will happen only if the employee wants it to happen. Only when employees internalize the meaning of excellence, recognize an authentic corporate commitment to excellence, and see the value to them in delivering excellence performance will they bring it to fruition.

It's time to recognize a new way to work with and energize people to bring out their best. If our goals are consistency, efficient processes, and obedient employees, we can keep on doing the same-old thing. But if our goal is excellence, top-down management tools and methods are invalid. It is time for a new management model.

The New "E"?

Several years ago, I hired Jeff (not his real name)—a young, ambitious MBA graduate—to work at my company. Jeff made quite an impression on my colleagues and me. He seemed to have the attitude we were looking for. During the interview process, Jeff asked all the right questions, he seemed to be sincerely interested in our work, and he provided us with excellent references. To ease his way into the company, the first assignment I gave him was a simple one that seemed to be a perfect fit given his previous experience. I wanted him to feel that he was making a contribution right away, and therefore, could feel at home with us. A week into Jeff's employment, I started to notice that his work was completely off the mark, not at all in line with what we'd originally agreed upon. We sat down together, I explained the assignment again, and we discussed a corrective course of action. A week later, the problem persisted, and everything we had talked about was being ignored. After four weeks of these persistent problems and few results, we convened for a serious discussion.

Jeff, who was aware of my growing discomfort with his performance, requested the opportunity to take the lead in the discussion, and I agreed. "I have needs," he started out. "I have emotional needs that I feel are not being fulfilled here. I need warmth and emotional support. I feel as though you are not dedicating enough time to support my emotional needs." He felt he should not have been given a project so early in his employment, and that in a "normal" situation, he would be deliverable-free for 6 to 8 months so that he could "absorb the environment."

It took me some time to digest the message Jeff had so eloquently articulated. He was convinced of his position and requested a protracted period during which we would fulfill his needs before we actually pressured him with real work, projects, and deliverables. After giving it much thought, I realized that Jeff had come to us devoid of a sense of responsibility. Rather, he had come with a sense of entitlement, one that more senior employees might have been expected to develop after a history of contributing to the company. Jeff expected such a normally "earned" entitlement on Day One.

Welcome to the world of the entitled employee. They seek the big "E"—which stands for not excellence but entitlement. These employees are not ready to assume responsibility, but they are quick to transfer it to others. After speaking to several headhunters, I concluded that Jeff was not the exception but the rule—the *emerging* rule.

In addition to the jaded employees many companies must deal with today, a new problem is looming. As we face an aging workforce and a shortage of qualified new employees, our challenges are being accelerated. We are replacing baby boomers with just plain babies. We are trading a sense of responsibility for a sense of entitlement. As a result, we are dramatically reducing the organizational capacity to deliver excellence and to differentiate lines of business. Without people who are willing to take responsibility, organizations will not be able to deliver superior results. As we develop new methods for managing and nurturing excellence, we must recognize that the audience is harder to please than ever.

Our hiring and selection criteria must focus on bringing in excellence-capable employees at the same time as we weed out applicants who come to us with expectations of entitlement. New ways of distinguishing the right people from lesser candidates need to be developed. Obedience and following the rules are increasingly irrelevant at a time when personal

Daily Choices determine the future and competitiveness of the organization. A penchant for serving and delighting customers, a connection to the organization's mission, and a personal commitment to excellence are more important than ever. If the people you hire are inherently unwilling and simply demanding instead, they will not offer excellence as part of their performance. Recognizing and weeding out those who exhibit a sense of entitlement during the hiring process is essential to your firm's excellence performance. Finding people who are willing to take responsibility is more critical then ever, and as a result, the competition for these candidates becomes more intense every day.

Imagine two employees we'll call Amy and John. Both have a track record of performance. Amy always meets her deadlines and delivers projects beyond expectations. You can count on her. John's performance is predictable as well. For every project assigned to him, he meets the deadline but never at the expected level of quality. While you can take a report from Amy and send it straight to your boss without hesitation, John's report will always need additional work. When you are ready to assign the next critical project, who will you choose? Amy, of course. And by giving Amy the project and continuing to employ John, you send Amy the message that "mediocrity pays."

To nurture an environment of excellence, you not only need to hire the right employees, you must eliminate the wrong ones. Tolerating poor performance by some workers will impact your top performers, dragging them down, or more likely, encouraging them to find work elsewhere, where excellence is expected and rewarded.

Generation Why?

Much has been written about "Generation Y" workers and their lack of commitment to their jobs. Yes, as a generation, these young people seem to possess a strongly noncommittal attitude, but these days, that attitude is not limited to any one age group. It is pervasive within the workplace as cynicism prevails, the result of too many disappointments and rampant mediocrity. I call this larger, more amorphous group "Generation Why." As in *why* should I do it, and what's in it for me?

This is not a small semantic change. In defining Generation Why, we move from an age group to a lifestyle group. This group encompasses all those cynical and skeptical employees who, regardless of when they were born, want to know, "Why should I care? Why should I try my best? Why should I bother to deliver excellence? Why is it worth *my* time?"

So, managers now face a new challenge: providing a strong answer to why. Many are not prepared for this, having long focused on the *how* and *when*, as opposed to either *why* or *what*. These managers have always dispensed orders and instructions without explaining them. Times have changed. Today, if you seek to nurture excellence, you will need to master the why.

It is only through your ability to articulate the big picture and the logic of the actions that you will be able to connect with and maximize the performance of Generation Why workers. The "just do it" approach doesn't cut it anymore.

Will it take longer to engage in conversation around the why? In all likelihood it will but the results will justify the time and effort you invest. In a world where employees are increasingly entitlement-focused, motivating them to do their best is easier said than done. Before they commit to a Daily Choice to deliver excellence, they will demand to know why they should make the effort. We must engage employees in a conversation about the benefits to *them* to show that choosing excellence is in alignment with their personal goals.

The managers who succeed in creating the right environment—those who can lead and motivate employees to excellence performance—are the managers who will win in the marketplace. You can be one of them. By unleashing the power of *why*, you will engage employees and obtain a level of commitment that supports the Daily Choice for excellence.

Upside-Down Management

With the ground rules of management changing when it comes to excellence, a completely new set of management tools is needed. Of the old management tools, "control" was the key. Processes and procedures were designed to control employee performance. Managers viewed performance through adherence to processes that allowed managers to hold employees accountable to a uniform performance level.

In sharp contrast, the excellence performance domain provides a clear shift of power from executives to employees. Excellence is subject to employee choice. Processes are tools to be used as needed: When the challenge presented fits the process at hand, employees should follow the process to delight customers. However, in cases where the process does not fit the problem, employees need to use discretion to customize and tailor their actions to meet the customer's needs. In these situations, employees are the primary assets, the process subservient to them. It is the employee's choice how and even *whether* to use processes, since the main goal is not adherence to procedure but rather to delight customers and deliver a complete experience.

A few readers will find these statements difficult to accept. The Six Sigma and lean manufacturing movements are entrenched, counting tens of thousands of consultants and practitioners as their followers. While rigid adherence to process is strongly advocated by the loyal soldiers of these movements, without employee discretion the result is a one-size-fits-all model that, in fact, fits relatively few of us. As customers accentuate their differences and demand individualized experiences, one-size-fits-all is not the answer. Thus, we must empower our employees.

A manager may be able to fire an employee but that is the extent of his power. He cannot make the employee deliver excellence unless she chooses to do so. Excellence is entirely optional on her part. This dramatic shift in power from obedience to performance-at-will reflects a new, upside-down management concept. Everything that was on top is now at the bottom and vice versa.

If the new world of excellence demands employee willingness, the question is whether it can be institutionalized. Can you actually manage excellence that has employee choice at its core? The answer is "Yes," but not in the old traditional ways. Excellence cannot be institutionalized the way processes are, with direction from above. Excellence *can* be institutionalized by providing fertile ground for superior performance to flourish.

Creating an environment that invites, entices, and supports such performance is the way to make excellence an everyday behavior in an organization. Just as a basketball coach cannot mandate success on the court, neither can the new excellence manager. The coach can guide his players and provide a productive environment, but the team's ultimate performance is up to each player. The team is in charge of the result. Similarly, an advertising executive cannot dictate that her creative director come up with a brilliant idea. She can provide a fun and stimulating environment, but the result is subject to the employee's choice. If he is inspired, the brilliant ideas will come naturally—and plenty of them, perhaps more than the firm can possibly follow up on. But if he is not engaged, no matter how many hours he spends in meetings or staring at his computer, the likelihood of excellence is slim to none.

Excellence is the opposite of top-down management, and executives who seek excellence must recognize this in the way they interact with their employees. Instead of being old-school bosses, they need to be nurturers and persuaders. Although excellence cannot be managed, it can be planted, grown, and cultivated. In a properly conducive environment, it will grow naturally. The role of managers must transform from one of keeping employees focused on mechanical tasks to one of creating environments that bring the best out of their employees *naturally*.

Persuading your employees that excellence is good for them is a primary dimension of your new role. Selling them on why excellence performance will allow them to be better, more satisfied individuals will go a long way toward realizing the excellence performance potential of the organization, as well as serving the organization's agenda. This persuasion starts with an inspiring mission. Employees need to see how their work can make a difference, and focusing on the positive impact their actions have on customers often presents the most compelling mission. Understanding how our work affects others can inspire us and turn even the most routine task into a source of great pride and personal satisfaction. Your employees need to see for themselves the value of unleashing the excellence within them. By creating and communicating a powerful mission and demonstrating employees' ability to make a difference, you can create the fertile ground for their Daily Choices—choices for excellence performance.

Coaching employees about excellence performance may not easy, but the rewards are great. Anyone can establish clear lines of authority and convince others to follow them for a paycheck, but it requires tremendous pluck, tact, caring, and skill to inspire someone to do more than what's required, to go above and beyond. There is no process that can be followed to force anyone to achieve excellence every day. Only you—mission leader, chief persuader, coach, and nurturer—can make it happen.

The Entrepreneurial Manager

I made an interesting observation while researching the upside-down management pyramid: The larger the company, the smaller the individual feels in terms of his ability to have an impact. Conversely, the smaller the organization, the more powerful the individual feels in terms of his ability to make a difference. It appears that a company's size and individual impact are operating in a zero sum game: The more one will gain, the less the other will have. When companies are in their infancy, with relatively few employees and little recognition in the marketplace, their capacity for excellence is almost limitless. The sense of responsibility employees feel, combined with their enthusiasm in contributing to the success of something worthwhile, creates a powerful force for excellence. When employees believe they are making a difference they willingly and joyously make a Daily Choice for excellence. For these workers, excuses are not an option; making excuses doesn't even cross their minds.

As a company grows and becomes established, its position in the marketplace solidifies and becomes an important factor in its success. During this period of growth, as staff is ramped up and a company becomes recognized as "large," employees begin to feel smaller. Many individuals who once felt the company's success was sitting squarely on their shoulders now find themselves becoming part of increasingly complex processes and see the level of responsibility they once enjoyed being diminished daily. They feel the company has changed and that one price of its success is a lack of appreciation for those who made it happen. It appears that the company will keep growing with or without them and, even worse, the executives don't seem to care. Before long, these employees no longer feel they are a part of the firm's success and, as a result, they begin to make different choices, easier choices—only to discover that no one even notices the level of their performance. The talk in the halls and in meetings is no longer about the achievements of those who built the firm. Instead, conversation revolves around how strong the brand is, and how the company is going to make a killing on its I.P.O.

What's happened is that the company has shifted its epicenter from excellence performance to the abstract power of the brand. Its leaders have forgotten what brought them to this stage of success: their employees' Daily Choices for excellence.

At some companies, the shift is pursued consciously, as executives obsessed with the bottom line take charge. These financial geniuses take over after years of viewing the organization through spreadsheets and graphs. They have spent most of their careers in isolation, never dealing with customers. As their influence grows, the organization is increasingly seen as a set of numbers. They demand adherence to new policies and protocols. To these executives, the essence of a business is not the accumulated experience of its people, but rather, it's the rate of financial growth that can be achieved through optimized processes.

In other firms, the shift from people to brand-centricity occurs almost unconsciously. The execs at these companies don't even notice the damage they are causing by promoting the abstract concept of brand power over and above the achievements of their employees. They may be unaware of the unintended consequences, but that doesn't change the ugly result.

Whether it's done consciously or not, the damage is the same. The bigger the perceived brand and the fatter the company's revenues, the more insignificant the individual employee is going to feel. This phenomenon has a direct and negative impact on a company's capacity for excellence. When brand becomes the end-all and be-all, employees—even while they may feel a certain pride in the brand's success—develop a tacit understanding that their performance is a secondary, perhaps insignificant factor. At this point, they see that forces beyond their control will decide the fate of the company and even their own destinies. As they begin delivering process-centric performance, choosing consistency over excellence, the accumulated impact slowly but surely depreciates the very brand the company is betting on for its long-term success.

As we approach the development of an upside-down management structure, it is critical to redefine the brand and its relative strength—not in abstract measures defined by ad agencies, but by the Daily Choices of employees. In spite of what many managers believe, the successful brand is not a matter of creative manipulation of the customer's perception. It is not a reflection on ad spending or the creativity of a corporation's marketing programs. Instead, the successful brand is a matter of genuine experience resulting from excellence performance. It is directly linked to the performance of each employee.

We must restore individual employee performance to its former and rightful place at the epicenter of the organization. Whatever the company considers as its intellectual property now, the definition needs to be expanded. The real intellectual property—the distinguishing factor that drives company loyalty—is the excellence performance of each employee and the cumulative impact of their efforts. Through thousands of Daily Choices, a strong brand is built—and built to last. Such a brand is not a matter of promises and perceptions created by ad agencies and marketers. A brand like this is a result of the organization's employees and their repeated, surprising, willingly provided delivery of excellence. Managing this delivery is the essence of the upside-down management pyramid.

We have all been taught that necessity is the mother of invention. Some of the world's greatest innovations have come about because an individual could not find what he needed, and then went ahead and developed it. Small companies enjoy a high level of innovation and creativity precisely because they are small. Many of the great entrepreneurs of the last 50 years have said that they were most effective when they had fewer than 10 employees on the payroll. Small companies may lack the resources of their larger competitors, but they compensate for it with agility, creativity, and innovation. Managers in smaller companies treat their employees as individuals and create a thriving environment for excellence largely because they have no other choice. They don't have a strong brand to carry them through difficult times, or revenue streams that will continue to flow even if all their best employees are hired by competitors.

There is good news for these small companies: The characteristics of entrepreneurial managers are particularly conducive to the upside-down management paradigm. Reliance on individual commitment and creativity, rather than dependence on resources and processes, makes entrepreneurial managers more successful in obtaining excellence performance.

If you choose to lead your team as an entrepreneurial group, exploiting every opportunity to empower your people, you will inspire excellence performance. Working under various constraints and with limited resources is no different for the manager in a large organization than for his small-business counterpart. Both have internal or external forces outside their control that influence work conditions. A strong focus on mission-based impact that is the result of your actions will align everyone and enable them to see beyond the obstacles. By adopting an entrepreneurial mentality and focusing on the people, you can lead and influence. Managers in large companies can develop the upside-down management skills required to drive their teams from mediocrity to excellence.

Embrace any limitation or difficulty as a catalyst to help you form creative solutions—as a challenge that can spark innovation, change the ground rules, and provide you with an edge and a means to deliver excellence to your customers. Remember that the greatest innovations of all have come as the result of necessity and scarcity.

"We Just Do"

While working at HP, I always tried to remind my staff of the need to center our focus on the impact we make on people's lives. We examined our performance and designed new rules, which we all committed to follow. One of those rules was responding to every customer request within two hours. It was not easy because our resources were extremely limited, even for a large corporation. (And, in fact, a 24-hour response was considered acceptable by many of our customers.)

Carly Fiorina, HP's CEO at the time, once confronted Bill, a member of my staff, challenging the two-hour response rule. "How can you possibly do it?" she asked. "This is an impossible objective." Bill's response was, "We just do." For him, it was the most natural thing in the world. He wasn't concerned with processes or limitations; he knew why it was important and he acted on it. He did not have a 5-inch-thick strategy plan to guide him. All he had was a laminated card, the size of a business card—a card that every member of my staff carried at all times—that stated our commitment.

Fly the Server

When a division of Siemens in Germany wanted to try our HP software, they needed a loaner server to conduct the test. Erik, a 20-year HP veteran, was based out of the HP office in Brussels and was assigned to spend most of his time working with Siemens on the project. Despite multiple attempts, pleas, and pressure, Erik failed to obtain the loaner server fast enough to meet Siemens's needs.

Erik was suddenly facing the Daily Choice. He could very easily respond to the customer with the saga of his attempts and an apology for the delay, taking the easy way out. He could demonstrate that, in spite of his (well-documented) efforts, the system simply did not work. Instead, remaining true to his personal commitment to the customer, Erik made the choice for excellence. He took one of his own servers from the Brussels office, flew to Germany, and handed it to the surprised Siemens staff.

Consumed with doing the right thing for his customer, Erik didn't take the time to request approval for his trip or to ask for permission to take an item of internal HP property and loan it to a customer. He simply acted on his personal conviction of excellence. He responded to the challenge in the way he wanted others to respond to him, were he ever in a similar situation.

Neither Bill nor Erik had ever done things like this before our team made the commitment to excellence. Each had worked for HP for many years but never dared to take such an extreme risk ("extreme" in the context of their existing departments). These were solid employees who always followed policy and received consistently high marks in the area of compliance with "corporate and team strategy and objectives." When presented with the opportunity to excel, independently and with the benefit of a nurturing environment of excellence, they discovered that they could rise to greatness. It was not a question of excellence capacity; it was a matter of being placed in an environment that allowed their capacities to be utilized, strengthened, and encouraged. Bill and Erik delivered superior service not because they were told to do it, but because they wanted to do it. For these employees, with whom I have been privileged to work, excellence became a personal matter—a matter of a Daily Choice that they alone could make.

When I realized that excellence was not something I could order people to do, I had to switch my position. Instead of being a boss, I became a servant, and a proud one at that. I realized that my division's excellence was the accumulation of the performance of all my employees. Our choice to deliver excellence—every day, in every interaction—and to raise the level of service we provided reflected directly on the overall performance of the division. We decided that we were not a top-down brand but a bottom-up performance team. We were as good as the total of our individual choices to provide exceptional service. As a result,

I had to switch my own traditional mode of operation, serving my employees so they could deliver excellence to our customers in return.

Excellence and the Art of Persuasion

To maximize the excellence potential of your organization, first stop focusing on salaries. Every one of your employees (especially the good ones) can find another job that pays more. Reducing work as a way to pay the bills will not inspire any of your employees to reach higher or to go above and beyond. To inspire them, you need to embrace upside-down management and actually start nurturing and stop managing.

The management tools that have been long regarded as fundamental are, today, the anti-tools of excellence. These old tools may allow you to reach parity but not excellence. Excellence requires asking your people to do certain things not because they have to obey (old management tools), but because they are inspired to do them.

According to *Dilbert* creator Scott Adams, "The least competent people become managers specifically because we do not want them to do the important work." This quote aptly illustrates how many of your employees may perceive you. It also indicates the level of commitment your employees have toward you when you are part of the old management paradigm. If your employees have this attitude, you have little if any chance of achieving your corporate objectives, from innovation to great customer service to operational excellence to risk-taking, or any other critical strategic goal. Who wants to work for or follow one of the least competent persons in the organization?

To assess your own management style, you need only ask yourself one question: "Why should they trust me?"

If the answer has to do with your power and position, you are managing with the old tools. If the answer is that you make them more successful and provide them with an environment to excel and maximize their potential, then you are nurturing, not managing. To be competitive in the future, companies can't count on the compliance and obedience of their employees. They need leaders who make people *do* great things because they *want* to do great things. This stands in stark contrast with Adams's definition.

Those who lead people to do what they want to do and to do it well nurture excellence. To achieve this we need the most, not the least, competent people. We need people who will be automatically respected by their peers. Any manager can engender *fear* in his subordinates (old management), while relatively few can achieve *respect*. Thus, the most powerful answer to the question, "Why should they trust you?" is "Because they respect you and your competence."

You are at the service of your employees. They see value in following your lead. Your people trust you because you bring value to their work and allow them to outperform their own perceived capabilities. Just about anyone will trust you in any setting if you encourage them, allow them to fail graciously, and enable them to excel.

In Chapter 7, we'll look at what it means to serve your employees and the leadership skills you'll need to do it right.

CHAPTER 7

Leading Your People to Excellence

Serving Your Employees

I've said that to achieve excellence, you need to turn your management style upside down. What does that really mean?

As a top-down manager, you act as the ultimate answer dispenser and problem-solver. You give your employees detailed instructions on how to do their jobs and answer every conceivable question. This management style may be widely accepted and encouraged in the workplace, but the problem is that employees narrow the scope of their potential actions and learn to stop thinking for themselves. They come to rely on you to have all the answers and to make every decision. As a result, they can no longer make a personal Daily Choice for excellence.

Leaders who create excellence all around them are the opposite of answer-dispensing machines. They foster an environment where employees are permitted and encouraged to make decisions and take risks, and, in the process, create excellence. These managers are not there to answer but rather to ask. They "train" their employees to handle any and all questions by giving them the power to create their own answers. As leaders, they don't see answering questions as their job; their role is about serving employees in ways that empower them to take charge.

To achieve this level of commitment to excellence through service to your employees, you need to recognize one major obstacle: your ego. Yes, ego is a necessary element of leadership. It is the driving force for many leaders, enabling them to assume more and more responsibility. On the other hand, an out-of-control ego can obviously hurt a manager's effectiveness. Managers who bring deeply rooted personal insecurities to leadership positions are known to feed their egos through bossing people around. Now that's top-down management at its worst. The insecure, power-obsessed, ego-driven manager will never successfully adopt a mindset of serving the employee and is therefore incapable of nurturing excellence performance.

Self-confident leaders, on the other hand, bring a positive ego to the employee relationship. These managers are comfortable with the role of serving their people. They view serving and nurturing employees as a privilege, not as a sign of weakness. They focus their efforts on creating influence rather than on seizing power. This service mode inspires excellence.

As a manager at HP, the role of serving my people was always a key to my relationship with them. I saw it as a privilege. I admit that, at the beginning, my newfound power was somewhat blinding. Most of us will bask in the first few moments of glory after attaining a new position at the top, but we quickly realize that we are now responsible for the success of a much larger community—that the "glory" is really just more responsibility. To get our jobs done, we need to get out of self-centric mode and start serving our people so they, in consequence, can focus on servicing their customers.

As a servant of my employees at HP, I defined my role as a combination of the following five key factors:

1. Extending their objectives beyond their comfort zone

2. Removing obstacles to performance

3. Providing tools for performance

4. Allowing room for mistakes

5. Recognizing and celebrating excellence

By stretching their objectives beyond their comfort zone, I provided my people with challenges. They had butterflies in their stomachs when they accepted their new objectives, but the challenge let them tap into the innate need to prove themselves. In cases where an individual doubted his ability to accomplish the objective, I pushed him to try. When success resulted, it was exhilarating. Discovering that you are capable of "more and better" is the greatest reward, and it more than compensates for what it takes to get there.

Early on, I learned that employees tend to underestimate their own capabilities. Sometimes they do it deliberately. Operating in your comfort zone can be easy and effortless. You assure yourself easy success ("I can do that with my eyes closed"). But the comfort zone is boring, and boredom does not lead to excellence. When you challenge employees to get outside their comfort zones, they become alert, engaged, and excited about the potential to deliver something new. Meeting a new challenge boosts an employee's confidence and reinforces her commitment to excellence performance.

Great managers focus on helping their people achieve their stretched objectives, not by doing their jobs for them, but by removing obstacles over which they have no control. Dealing with corporate bureaucracy is debilitating even for the most enthusiastic and committed employee. Often, staff must deal with conflicting agendas, rules, and personal objectives that make superior individual performance seem almost impossible. In assuming the role of "Chief Bureaucracy Removal

Officer" in my department at HP, I freed my employees so they could focus on the customer and drive their performance to the maximum.

Although it has long been my personal conviction that Chief Bureaucracy Removal Officer is among the most important of management roles, I didn't recognize how critical the role was until I conducted a global Customer Experience study in 2006. This annual study, which polls hundreds of marketing and customer service leaders worldwide, is designed to survey customer experiences and its linkage to employee experience. Our questions are geared toward understanding the ability of employees to perform their assigned tasks and responsibilities within the corporate environment. In the last three annual surveys, only an average 34 percent of responding executives agreed that their people have the tools and authority to service customers. In the absence of tools and authority (and relevant information is an integral part of that kit), employees are not able to make a Daily Choice for excellence.

If you don't provide your employees with the tools and information they need to excel, you not only make it virtually impossible for them to deliver excellence, you send the dispiriting message that the company does not value their work. If they lack the necessary tools and information, employees are unable to make educated decisions and take calculated risks. They simply cannot justify their decisions. As a result, they succumb to the rules that protect them from retribution in the event a decision comes back to haunt them, often in the form of a customer complaint. For managers to awaken the excellence of their employees, they must remove bureaucratic obstacles and provide the tools, information, and authority employees need to perform.

The following story illustrates the power of providing the necessary tools and allowing employees to make decisions even at the risk of failure.

Summer Santa

An "extra" from an airline has become as rare as chocolate on a hotel bed pillow. With the airline industry struggling for profitability, today's carriers skimp wherever possible to minimize their cost. One consequence is that airlines' willingness to address problems and be generous in the event of mistakes has become virtually extinct. Fortunately, there are always exceptions to the rule.

On a Virgin Atlantic flight to London, I witnessed a problem and a startling way of proactively addressing it. As the aircraft took off, I was ready to start working. As soon as the announcement permitting the usage of electrical devices was made, I turned on my laptop. After I had been working for a few minutes, the flight attendant came over and said: "Sir, our on-board entertainment system is not working. We are truly sorry for the inconvenience. Would you like to receive 75 pounds sterling in duty-free products or 10,000 miles credited to your frequent flyer account?"

My first reaction was that this was some kind of a joke, but to my amazement, the offer was in earnest. The flight attendant approached the passengers one-by-one with the proposal. I opted for the duty-free products, interested to see how serious the airline was about this. My guess was that I would receive a coupon good only for products in a remote, difficult-to-reach shop. I was pleasantly surprised when the attendant handed me the duty-free catalog and allowed me to make my selections then and there. If Santa Claus was real, I felt I was seeing him in action (despite the summer heat) in the garb of a Virgin Atlantic flight attendant.

My curiosity was piqued, and I went forward to discuss the matter with the purser. I was sure that it was either her last day with the airline or she was simply suicidal. She explained that it had been her decision to offer passengers either duty-free items or extra frequent flyer miles. Economy class passengers were offered 3,000 miles or 25 pounds sterling in duty-free products, economy-plus passengers were offered 5,000 miles or 35 pounds sterling in duty-free, and business-class passengers were offered 10,000 miles or 75 pounds sterling for the duty-free option.

"Are you following the rules?" I asked. "Is this procedure documented in the manual?"

"No," she said and explained that she was not acting based on predefined rules. Instead, she had used the knowledge the company empowered her with, and used it wisely to make a common-sense decision: She knew that every complaint cost the company at least 25 pounds sterling to process, even before the cost of resolution. She also knew that frequent flyer miles are the cheapest form of compensation. By applying this knowledge, she was able to come up with a proactive resolution not only to avoid customer disappointments (and, ultimately, complaints) but to delight them, even in the face of a broken entertainment system. By understanding the customer segmentation based on the class of ticket purchased, she was able to appropriately differentiate, and by providing a choice of duty-free product or frequent flyer miles, she shifted the burden of the decision to the customers rather than dictating a take-it-or-leave-it offer.

Knowledge had empowered this airline employee to deliver excellence. The routine approach would have been, "Sorry. To complain, call our customer service line," but she opted for a strong solution over a weak retreat. She hadn't personally created the problem, yet she took responsibility for the solution. She did not focus on the functional aspects of the problem (e.g., filling out the form), but rather, she focused on its impact on others—specifically, on *her* customers. She was only able to do what she did by knowing the numbers and, therefore, having the confidence that her decision was economically justified. Without this knowledge, it's likely she would have defaulted to a stock response that would no doubt have created hundreds of irritated customers and cost the airline much more than the gifting had.

At the end of her workday, the purser documented her action in the flight log and Virgin Atlantic management subsequently accepted it. (I know this because during our conversation, I asked her to let me know the response of her supervisors to her "generous decision.") This story shows that providing employees with the right tools, information, and authority makes business sense, because it allows them to make educated decisions, prevent risks, and maximize opportunities. Most importantly, it frees them to avoid compromise and aim higher.

Live in the Customer's Shoes

In Chapter 3, I described the Experience Gap Analysis (EGA) research, indicating that the majority of employees fail to deliver superior performance because they do not fully understand customer expectations. These workers tend to view customers as recipients of goods and services, not as human beings with hopes and dreams. They perform based on their own preconceived notions, which are typically not in alignment with the customer's own definition of excellence. As the cliché goes, customers do not need a drill, they need a 3-inch hole. Excellence does not deliver functional features; it delivers a complete, emotionally engaging resolution that takes the problem away completely. It is problem resolution combined with a human touch in a surprisingly effortless process. Customers notice and appreciate this level of performance.

To address and correct the perception gap, the first step is to define what excellence looks like to the customer. What is her standard of excellence? The operative definition must adhere to the recipient's expectations, not to those of the employees who deliver on them. In creating a definition based on the customer's expectations, we put a standard in place that allows us to pursue a legitimate solution. Following this definition stage, managers need to create special education programs to help every employee better understand their customers and how they interact with the company's products or services. First and foremost, employees need to be able to visualize the recipient's definition of excellence.

As an abstract term, excellence is subject to personal interpretation. An education program that focuses on customers—their hopes, dreams, lifestyles, and excellence expectations—will allow employees to see excellence through the eyes of the beholder. The program should directly address the specific problems customers are trying to solve through the company's products and services. The entire surrounding lifestyle of the customer needs to be taught to each employee so that he can differentiate his service, personalizing it and letting the customer feel a much needed and caring human touch.

Most employee training programs today address the functional skills of employees, yet they fail to educate them on the uniqueness of their customers or on the importance of recognizing each customer's unique needs, hopes, and dreams. These are the very factors that motivate someone to purchase and use your products or services. It is the ultimate outcome, as opposed to features and functions, that impacts a customer's thinking most and leads her to prefer your products and services to those of your competitors. Traditional training treats all customers the same, viewing them through the "one size fits all" lens of the products and services they receive. When employees fail to recognize the diversity of their customers, they miss opportunities to react to the wide variety of needs these customers want to address.

To deliver excellence, employees need to get below the surface and really understand their customers. This requires training and hands-on experience that allows them to visualize and understand "a day in the life" of the customer. They need to know by heart the customer's work pressures, frustrations, hopes, dreams, and fears. Only when a complete profile of a customer (as a human being) is painted can an employee adapt his performance to resolve the unique needs of the individual.

Training needs to be transformed from functional "skill drills" into full-fledged customer education courses. Customers need to be transformed—as they are perceived by employees—from wallets with budgets to real people with needs and feelings. Until these transformations are achieved, we cannot expect employees to appreciate the potential and power of excellence performance.

Empowered to Make the Right Decision?

Empowerment is a strange management concept. Every manager swears he empowers his people, yet no employee ever acknowledges being empowered. One reason for the disconnect is that "empowerment" means something different to the two groups. I define empowerment as the ability to own an issue and solve the problem. If an employee cannot make a decision to solve a problem without approval from a higher-level manager, he is not empowered. In such a situation, the employee is the equivalent of a secretary taking notes for the boss to use in making a delayed, distanced, profit-centered decision.

In spite of the popular perception by employees, empowerment is not about free rein to spend. Instead, it is about greater responsibility. Empowering people is not the same as giving them a license to spend recklessly. The power to make decisions comes with the power to be held accountable for those decisions. Without accountability, empowerment is recklessness. When they discover this unfortunate reality, many employees become reluctant to be empowered: They are not ready to assume the responsibility, the accountability that is required for empowerment to work.

"What is wrong with some stupid people who follow the rules?" I was once asked at an executive seminar. I admired the person who dared to ask it, because he expressed what was on the minds of many other managers who listened to the concepts, nodded courteously, but had no plan to implement anything I was talking about. I have no doubt that some of them actually believed in "the-stupid-people-who-follow-the-rules" management model. This type of manager is convinced that employing obedient, non-thinking employees is the best way to run a business.

One reason for management's reluctance to truly empower employees has to do with a control issue. Many managers are not comfortable relinquishing control to those they consider inferior or simply do not trust. Some of these reluctant managers go as far as to hire people who will clearly *not* be able to assume any additional responsibility, then use employee lack of readiness as a shield for their "bigger and wiser" influence. By and large, managers are very comfortable with the top-down management structure in which they are on top and "the stupid people who follow the rules" are on the bottom.

So, one might ask, what's wrong with "the stupid people who follow the rules?" (First of all, if they are truly stupid, we should avoid hiring them and wasting the company's money.) Employee performance is limited to a fixed number of hours per day during which they perform two types of work: routine tasks and exception-type activities. When dealing with exceptions, employees add value by solving problems that rules and procedures do not address. They bring creativity and caring to "exception to the rule" situations. Because these kinds of situations offer opportunities for leadership, risk-taking, creativity, and innovation, they often represent the finest moments of any employee's career. Stupid people who follow the rules need not apply.

Then, there is routine work. Here, employees can actually contribute errors rather than value: If a transaction is *truly* routine, an automated system will do it more accurately than a human being every time. With routine work, the stupid people who follow the rules will miss every opportunity to add a human touch and personalization and, therefore, will fail to differentiate the company through excellence.

So, it is clear that stupid people who follow the rules are not the answer to differentiated performance in either routine or exception work. By creating an obedient performance environment, we will cultivate this mindless way of following the rules and miss the greatest potential contribution of our people. Over time, such environments even strip intelligent people of the motivation and ability to make a difference.

The true value of employees is in exception-handling and adding excellence to routine work. The number of exceptions is growing quickly as customers increasingly demand customized resolutions to their problems on their terms. One-size-fits-all solutions are being replaced by tailor-made solutions in response to customers' requests. Exception handling is becoming a more significant aspect of employees' overall performance—precisely why we need human beings and not robots in the workforce. With the growing number of exceptions to deal with, employing stupid people who follow the rules is counter-productive to our goals of excellence. We need people who can make decisions and address thorny problems with aplomb. In other words, we need exceptional people, not stupid ones. And while we are taking the time to find these exceptional people, let's not forget that it will require exceptional management and true empowerment to deliver excellence while handling these many exceptions.

When we discuss empowering employees, an underlying assumption is that every individual wants to assume greater responsibility and is willing to be held accountable. Often this is not the case, and it takes two to tango. If we hired the wrong people or did not create an environment conducive to excellence, employees will tend to avoid assuming any additional responsibility. If your employees specialize in mechanical task completion, it's unlikely they are interested in taking on more responsibility. Accepting increased responsibility is usually a matter of choice and cannot be effectively mandated from the top.

Let's assume you have been given a major promotion under one condition: You need to assign a person from your group to take over your current role immediately and without any interruption to the business. How many of your employees would fit the bill? They may want your salary, but are they striving for your level of responsibility? Only in an excellence-focused, nurturing environment can this type of condition be fulfilled. Simply discussing the principle of empowering people does not ensure that anyone is going to accept empowerment. Your role as a manager, using an upside-down management paradigm, is to create the environment that will breed this type of behavior. Fortunately, it is the same environment that will breed excellence.

Permission to Fail

"In our company, everyone is empowered to make the right decisions."

This comment, presented to me by an eager client, offers the best illustration of the problem with empowerment I can provide. I hope you caught the absurd element in the statement. All employees are empowered to make the *right* decisions. Clearly, they are not permitted to make any *wrong* ones.

Imagine the manager of the New York Yankees telling his players, "From now on, it's all home runs or you're fired." It would be equally ridiculous to hear him saying, "If you don't hit a home run, do not bother to come back to the bench. You might as well pack up your stuff and leave." It's easy to see how absurd such a demand is in the context of baseball, or any other sport for that matter. Uncertainty is part of the game. The more often you come to the plate to swing at the ball, the greater the chances are that you will hit a home run. The fewer chances you take, the lower your chances to succeed. Mistakes are part of the game.

Some players may never hit a home run, but no matter what talent they are nurturing, they must have the permission to fail in order to discover how high they can reach.

In the game of business, we try to change the basic rules. Have you ever thought about the fact that a baseball player who fails 65 percent of the time will probably end up making it to the pros? That's right: A .350 average is phenomenal in major league baseball—that means not getting a hit 65 percent of the time. And yet, for our employees, we often set goals of 85 percent, 90 percent, or 95 percent success. What does this kind of expectation do to our excellence performance? We send a message to employees that mistakes are too risky and that they may lead to fatal repercussions. In such an environment, the organization will quickly succumb to mediocrity. People will be afraid to take chances or risk mistakes and, therefore, will default to inaction. They will procrastinate about critical decisions and cause the organization to miss important opportunities in the process. The overall performance of an organization with little to no mistakes is rooted in mediocrity and not excellence.

Think for a moment about how your organization accommodates failure. Do employees feel that failure is permitted? Do they feel that your expectations are humanly possible?

The question of permission to fail is not just a question of being nice to your employees. It raises a greater question of permitting them to take risks, to try new things in a safe environment, and to achieve and deliver excellence.

Mistake of the Month

While working with a division of a large German company, I proposed to demonstrate the company's commitment to excellence through a program I called "Mistake of the Month." Following the principles of employee of the month, the company would reward the best mistake of the month. Karl, an executive with the company, liked my idea and made it happen. One of his employees took a call from a customer late one evening. The customer had a request that was out of the scope of the employee's authority. No manager was available to approve it, so the employee took the risk and made the commitment to the customer anyway. The following day, we discovered that the commitment could not be honored due to some regulatory issues.

This employee had demonstrated both a commitment to customers and a willingness to take risks to delight them. (Behavior that signified excellence in Karl's mind.) So, Karl arranged a small party to celebrate the mistake. The employee was awarded a gift certificate and a special cake was ordered to mark the occasion. Various employees watched in disbelief. They could never have imagined a party for a mistake (can you?). But, at the same time, they were given a strong and immediate message: Mistakes are welcome here. As long as you take calculated risks and demonstrate commitment to customers, any mistakes will be respected as part of the success process.

When celebrating employee mistakes, we must focus on the right mistakes, not the ones that occur as the result of procrastination, inaction, or negligence. We want to reward mistakes that reflect commitment, a willingness to invest time and resources, the courage to take personal risks, and other positive patterns of behavior. As managers, our role is to encourage the type of performance that can result in success and excellence, and this requires accepting some mistakes. The cost of not making mistakes is much higher, because, simply put, a world without mistakes is a world without excellence.

Recognizing Excellence

Recognizing and celebrating excellence is tricky. The right celebrations will likely lead to widespread inspiration to reach even higher. The wrong celebrations will lead to complacency and, ultimately, to failure. Some organizations celebrate excellence frequently and arrogantly, as a form of boasting, believing it affirms their greatness. These types of celebrations are typically based on the firm's definition of excellence rather than the customer's, and it often seems that celebration is the goal and excellence merely a vehicle to get there. Frequent celebrations of this type will result in distorted definitions of success and, ultimately, missed business opportunities. After several years of this behavior, companies usually find themselves in trouble, facing tough competition and a shortage of ideas for restarting the excellence engine.

At the other end of the spectrum are the companies that never celebrate anything. Their mindsets range from "nothing we do is good enough" to "we don't know how to deliver success." While being aware of our weaknesses is important for all of us who want to do better, a defeatist attitude reflects low organizational self-esteem, which is as dangerous as hubris. When employees doubt their ability to deliver excellence, they make poor decisions, or simply avoid making decisions, and before long, the doubt becomes a self-fulfilling prophecy. If you do not make and follow through on the decisions that deliver excellence, you are not, in fact, delivering it. In failing to deliver excellence you reinforce your sense of inferiority, and so the vicious cycle continues.

The truth is that many organizations do deliver excellence but never stop to recognize it. Their employees eventually give up trying because "no matter what we do, it will never be good enough." Failing to recognize excellence—and to celebrate it—is not healthy. Organizations need to reinforce the message that excellence is expected and rewarded. Celebrating excellent performance helps employees visualize success.

Michael Dell was once quoted as saying that, at Dell, they celebrate in nanoseconds. The idea is that you celebrate success and then quickly move on to the next challenge. I am not sure that I buy into the nanosecond-party concept. Human beings need to time to reflect and plan for the future, and a well-conceived, unhurried public display of recognition helps in this introspection process. Such celebrations reinforce the organization's and the employee's capacity for excellence and encourage future high-caliber performances. However, while I'm not sure about the nanosecond celebrations, Dell's concept is valid: Use your excellence celebration not as an excuse to brag, but to inspire you to move on to the next challenge.

Recognition can be used as an educational and motivational tool that helps your employees aim higher and believe in their ability to deliver above and beyond what they have done before. In celebrating their superior performance, you send a message that the company does not take excellence for granted and provide incentive for every employee to excel.

Would You Go All the Way?

The pursuit of fun at work has become a trendy must-do for managers worldwide. Research shows that a relaxed work environment incorporating fun and humor makes most employees more creative and productive, and, of course, that is what we want them to be. (We'll do whatever crazy thing it takes to get the most out of our employees!)

One company that's often cited for its fun-in-the-workplace culture is Southwest Airlines. Southwest manages to get its employees engaged and motivated to the point that they actually share their enthusiasm with passengers. Business reporters love to cover the Southwest culture, which they often depict as the secret of the company's success in a brutally competitive market. Unfortunately, while other firms study Southwest's formula and try to copy its techniques for building a companywide commitment to excellence, they frequently fail to recognize that fun and humor do not come on demand. They are a result of employee choice supported by the company's principles, policies, and culture.

For starters, Southwest publicly and clearly identifies employees as its most important asset—above stockholders and even customers. If your firm is not ready to make a similar commitment to its employees, it's unlikely you will be able to create a culture of fun. When they are not supported by strong principles and policies, initiatives designed to make work more fun only reinforce a cynical view of the company. Employees know sincerity when they see it; if they are not being treated as true equals and recognized for their contributions to the company's success, management's feel-good initiatives will fall flat. Without a commitment to the critical principles that organizations like Southwest put in place to establish a nurturing environment for employees, then excellence, creativity, and fun will not take root. Instead, the situation will be analogous to putting lipstick on a pig. (Even with the lipstick, a pig is still a pig.) Only a sincere and authentic commitment to employees will work. Superficial attempts will be doomed to failure.

Another company frequently viewed as a benchmark is Nordstrom, famous for its customer service. In their book *The Nordstrom Way*, Robert Spector and Patrick D. McCarthy describe the simple, common-sense way in which the Nordstrom family runs the company. Examples include the chairman picking up rubbish rather than asking an employee to do it, and Nordstrom family members taking their own calls and personally answering their callers' questions. Unless you are ready to cheerfully pick up the rubbish, don't bother trying to imitate the best. If you manage your customer relationships through underlings, your chances of living the Nordstrom way are slim to none.

These examples wouldn't make good business sense if they did not have sound guiding principles behind them. Without such principles supporting your performance, the effort will be superficial and easily dismissed. Without genuine willingness on your part, a reciprocal commitment from your employees will not be gained. If you choose to benchmark other companies and replicate their successful practices, realize that you are not there yet, and that aspiring to such a high level of performance will require you to make bold, principle-based changes.

I Will Take the Cynic Over Any Other Employee

Imagine that it is staff meeting time. You are leading the meeting and going through the agenda. There is general agreement with all your suggestions, and the meeting is moving along well. But then there is a minor disruption—laughter from the back of the room. You look up to see Brian.

Brian is the ultimate cynic. He thrives on sarcasm and caustic humor (you would laugh at his jokes if they weren't about you). As the meeting has progressed, Brian has assumed his traditional role of cynical joker, offering derisive asides in response to your ideas and initiatives. His co-workers giggle as the cynical comments roll off his sharp tongue.

By this time, you have grown quite irritated with Brian and his disruptive behavior. You wish he would quiet down, show a little respect, and get with the program. But wait. Before you jump to conclusions about Brian's ability to be part of the team and to make a meaningful contribution to the projects at hand, you need to ask yourself the following questions:

- Do you really believe that the rest of your employees are fully committed to the agenda you presented in the meeting?

- Why didn't any staff member offer suggestions of his or her own?

- Was everyone so convinced by your arguments that they were simply left speechless?

- Are they ready to execute without having engaged in any real discussion?

- What are the chances that this agenda will be fully and enthusiastically implemented?

The truth is that the silent acceptance you experienced during the meeting was the sound of disengaged employees. Once upon a time, they had plenty to say, and you can be sure they still have opinions. This extends to your latest agenda: No doubt, some agree with it while some don't; some have questions, and others may be inclined to play the devil's advocate. Yet, they all kept their mouths shut. They heard you speak, but they did not engage with or absorb any part of what you were saying. Their main agenda was getting the meeting over with as quickly as possible. It's likely these people are so burned-out that they don't even want to bother anymore; they have tried many times and ultimately have given up. Their attitude is epitomized by the GenX catchphrase "Whatever."

Brian, on the other hand, is engaged. He has been listening and commenting. You may not like his style, but it would be a mistake to ignore his commitment. Though you may consider his commentary a negative one that you can do without, don't rush to conclusions. Stop for a second and think about Brian.

Like many cynics, Brian is a passionate individual who strives for excellence. He probably joined the company and your department because he believed in its vision and mission. He came to make a difference and apply his passion. Over time, as a result of various disappointing experiences with the firm, he became disenchanted and cynical. But a cynic is actually a positive person who channels his passion in a negative way, in the absence of positive outlets. Brian still believes in the company and wants to do the right thing, but he is looking for a meaningful opportunity. Unlike the many tongue-tied employees in your meeting who simply nodded in compliance, he still has the passion, and he wants the company and its initiatives to be successful.

As with many cynics, Brian is a great employee, but we have frequently let him down or even abused him. In spite of this, he still has it within him to deliver excellence. Meanwhile, the rest of your employees remain silent, playing zombies in their offices, hiding behind processes and excuses. Many of them may not be redeemable.

We have been conditioned to view attitudes like Brian's as negative and disruptive, but in the world of upside-down management, we seek excellence and not just consistency. In situations where we seek responsibility, not just the conduct of pre-formulated actions without accountability, the cynic is our man (or woman). For one thing, it is always easier to handle the bulls than to motivate the mules.

When I spoke about cynicism in Chapter 1, I described it as affecting our long-term competitiveness and ripping away our potential for excellence. Keep in mind that I was talking about *cynicism*, not about the *cynics*. Let's not confuse the illness with the sufferer. Our cynics have great potential, but their cynicism needs to be rerouted, and that is the task of our new manager. While the top-down manager will quickly seek to get rid of the cynic, the new coach will embrace him, challenge him, and provide him with a nurturing environment to perform. At the same time, the root cause of the employee's cynicism needs to be addressed and ultimately eliminated.

The noisiness of your staff meetings is an effective litmus test of your employees' readiness for excellence. How loud are they? How argumentative are the participants? If you think quiet staff meetings that bring quick agreement are desirable, think again. In the world of upside-down management, it is the louder and more argumentative meetings that matter.

Noisy, passionate meetings almost always produce the best ideas and solutions. To make this format work, permission to object and to express an opinion has to be consistently communicated. Employees need to know that regardless of where they stand in the corporate hierarchy, their ideas are welcome. Of course, we do not seek "loud" for its own sake, but for the sake of more open, passionate, and successful communication and decision-making. By the end of our meeting, agreement needs to be reached along with a plan of execution.

Tell Me a Story

It is difficult to define "excellence" before achieving it. In fact, when I ask seminar participants to imagine excellence, inevitably each has a different vision. For some, it's reaching the top of Mount Everest, for others, it's an Olympic medal. For one person, excellence is a Porsche; for another, it's his baby girl. Everyone has his own version of excellence, and in the absence of a common definition, an organization can be seen as a collection of great but disconnected ideals and intentions.

To create a common understanding of how to create excellence, companies can develop a repository of stories that embody their ideal of excellence. Each organization needs to build its own culture of excellence, where employees have a shared concept of what excellence is all about. If every employee runs with his own version of excellence, the company cannot harness the power of excellence synergy to create the desired level of human differentiation and customer loyalty.

Storytelling is almost the antithesis of the way businesses share information today. Everything we know is tightly packed into spreadsheets and pie charts. Each bit of information must be short, to the point, and go straight to the bottom line. By contrast, tomorrow's leaders must master the art of storytelling. They need to learn to tell inspirational stories that spark people's imaginations to what is possible. Frequently sharing stories in staff meetings, through companywide correspondence, and through one-on-one interactions will contribute measurably to the effectiveness of your communications. The more stories you tell, the greater your employees' grasp of what excellence means in the context of their organization. Sure, it may take longer than the five-minute PowerPoint presentation you're used to giving, but its impact will be much greater and longer lasting. People will remember your stories long after they've forgotten the facts and figures from that PowerPoint talk. (And, please, if you insist on using PowerPoint to help you tell a story, incorporate images that illustrate it.)

An organization's definition of excellence is dictated largely by the customers it serves. Knowing what is just "OK" for them vs. what they consider "great" is critical. This understanding of customers helps us define and build a detailed picture of excellence performance that every employee can internalize. A collection of excellence stories can be a powerful tool to illustrate to employees what excellence looks like. This collection should include dozens of stories geared toward both inspiring employees *and* showing how far excellence can go if we are willing to unleash our passion and place the customer at the center of all that we do.

Celebrating the Heroes

In my search for excellence stories and practices, I came across many corporate programs designed to recognize great customer service. I learned that they are typically conducted as a mandatory exercise with very little inspiration, as if someone in HR decided some kind of program was inevitable and deployed one reluctantly. One such program, however, stood in stark contrast to all the rest.

The Ron Hicks World Class Service Award program at HomeBanc was so inspiring that I could tell immediately it was not designed reluctantly but with commitment and enthusiasm. Unlike similar programs, HomeBanc designed its program with pride and believed it could really make a difference.

When I first received the details of the program from HomeBanc's Office of the Customer, I was handed a glossy four-color brochure featuring the photographs and personal stories of the 12 final-ists. The brochure was as beautifully designed as anything the company might have used to promote a key product or service. It was obvious that no effort had been spared to demonstrate to all employees that this recognition really mattered to the company. Here was an authentic focus on excellence, presented in living color.

Originally initiated in 1997, HomeBanc's award begins with the selection of a winner and a runner-up every month. At the end of the year, at the company's annual meeting, all monthly winners are invited to the stage and a random drawing is conducted. The winner and a guest receive an all-expenses paid trip to anywhere in the world.

In 1999, the award program was renamed after Ron Hicks, an asso-ciate who died in a car accident. Ron represented excellence to all who knew him. Colleagues described him as someone who inspired others to reach higher and achieve more. Six months after his death, customers still called his extension asking for assistance, demonstrating the depth of the relationships he had forged. Ron led by example, and HomeBanc wanted all its employees to aspire to the same type of excellence performance.

This award program shares similar features with other recognition programs. The monthly winner receives a specially designed pin and certificate, the CEO highlights her accomplishment in a meeting with all associates, and there is a monetary award. At the end of the year, however, HomeBanc really turns up the volume. Significant award money—ranging from $5,000 to $25,000—is presented to the annual winners, demonstrating the importance the bank places on excellence performance.

"Our most revered employee recognition program centers not around sales and unit volume, but around the unique and powerful delivery of world class service," according to Jamey Lutz, vice president of HomeBanc's Office of the Customer. "Ron Hicks epitomized service excellence, and it's only fitting that we celebrate his life through an award bearing his name."

By putting a face and a name to its award program, HomeBanc added a compelling human element. Celebrating the winners via a beautifully designed brochure is another unique way for the firm to demonstrate its commitment to excellence and to individual Daily Choices to create excellence. With approaches such as these, excellence is no longer faceless and abstract. It is not just a name. Excellence is represented by real, passionate people who have the power to inspire others. HomeBanc has succeeded in creating a new standard for these types of programs.

Excellence Enablement

Is it possible to institutionalize excellence? Not with traditional management practices, although by utilizing the roles of coach, nurturer, and server, managers can create a culture of excellence. Excellence cannot be mandated from above, but the right environment will encourage people to choose it.

Selecting excellence-capable people and avoiding entitlement people is the first critical step to building an excellence-capable organization. Defining the organization as the total of employee performance, rather than emphasizing profits and brand visibility, enables excellence. Defining excellence in relation to customer expectations, instead of corporate interpretations, will subject the organization to a higher standard and bring it closer to achieving its goals. An educational program that expands beyond products and procedures to encompass customers, their hopes and dreams, will help employees to understand what excellence is all about.

Enabling excellence through permission to perform is another critical step on the journey to realizing your organization's excellence capacity. Allowing employees to make mistakes and supporting them by removing obstacles to performance will empower them to make the Daily Choice for excellence. As managers, we must evolve to become "chief supporting officers" to our employees. And we need to provide, on an ongoing basis, the kind of working environment that encourages employees to make a habit of excellence.

To institutionalize excellence, our focus must be not only on our managers but on individual employees as well. After all, unleashing the organization's capacity for excellence is directly linked to each employee's ability to unleash his excellence capacity. How does an individual define personal excellence and make the Daily Choice in spite of challenges, obstacles, and distractions? As leaders, how can we avoid inertia and maintain a vital commitment to excellence and to superior performance? These are among the questions we will tackle in Chapter 8.

CHAPTER 8

Making Excellence Personal

When I Grow Up I Want to Be ...

When you were a child, what was your dream profession? What did you want to be when you grew up? The list of popular dream professions is long and diverse, including doctor, astronaut, police officer, scientist, rock star, actor, fireman, clergy, teacher, nurse, artist, lawyer, paramedic, dancer, athlete ... the list goes on.

It's interesting to note the common denominators of these desirable professions. Each offers an opportunity to touch people in a meaningful way. They are all about a wish to accomplish something far above average. Of course we want to live a meaningful life! As children we dream about ways to make a difference, to help others, and to express ourselves. Rather than passive roles, we are drawn to professions that reflect our hopes of becoming dynamic individuals making important, lasting contributions to society and the world. We don't want to be dependent, always on the receiving end. We want to be proactive, on the giving end. This giving may involve helping people in need or exciting and inspiring those around us through our personal accomplishments. In either case, we aspire to create admirable performance. We want to express our capacity for excellence. This giving, whether through assisting others or achieving breakthroughs, is the highest symbol of excellence in our innocent eyes.

No kid ever said "I hope to add value to shareholders," or "I wish I could make rich people richer, through hard, boring work." We do not get excited by statements encouraging us to increase the wealth of people who are already rich. Yet, firms often place the wealth of shareholders at the top of their corporate agendas, and then seem surprised when employees are not inspired to do their best. Children are not inspired by the promise of slaving away for others, and as adults, we are no different. We want to feel that our work makes a difference. We want others to see value in our efforts. Our passion will be given to activities that clearly result in something we can be proud of. So, when companies set their goals around shareholder value and return, they are setting up the environment in the company for anything but excellence. They are creating a context that does not inspire excellence performance, but rather inhibits it.

If you have any doubt at this point about the power of passion in driving people to excellence performance, just stop for a moment to consider the Linux operating system. Linux, which was started as a hobby project by a Finnish engineer, became a worldwide phenomena and a successful commercial product against all odds. It was created by committed people working without the "benefit" of a traditional organizational structure. It was built out of the personal commitment of individuals who did not need managers to tell them what excellence is or how to deliver it. A personal commitment and a willingness to be part of something great drove the excellence performance. Linux was created by people around the world, working on their own time, using the Internet as a shared project space. There were no bosses, no shareholders, no corporate mission statements, and no paychecks, which is the most impressive of all. These passionate volunteers created a popular and highly effective product that forced the world's leading software companies to spend millions to compete with it and gave birth to a multibillion-dollar market.

Basically, here's how it worked. Each participant contributed (on a purely volunteer basis) to the development of a feature or capability that added value to the base Linux technology. Each contributor imagined a new capability he believed Linux needed, and then went ahead and worked to deliver that functionality. Each person added to the technology and agreed that any other user could freely use his contribution. A combination of self-drive, a commitment to a cause, and countless invested hours by brilliant engineers resulted in a great product that became serious competition for the world's largest software company. And all these accomplishments were delivered without any of the participants being paid. They wanted to do it. They were proud to be part of it. They saw a way to deliver meaningful performance and chose to do it—and that, in a nutshell, is the definition of excellence.

The Linux community worked without a single manager to order people around. They had natural leaders but no manager was necessary to achieve this amazing accomplishment. The lesson here is that when people share a cause, when they believe in a project, fewer rules are better than more. When people only see a fraction of the full picture and are not being given the logic and purpose, they require in-depth instruction and management; their tendency will be to perform reluctantly. Too many rules kill the spirit and with it the commitment to excellence. Linux did the exact opposite and let the spirit lead. That's why it worked.

What we desperately need to create in order to achieve excellence performance is a meaningful mission to make a difference. Despite all the discouraging signals that corporations send with the "shareholder value" message, there are opportunities to achieve and make a difference in every task we do every day. Excellence is waiting for us everywhere in a multitude of opportunities. Everywhere, enclaves of people have learned to work the system (or work around it, if necessary) to achieve excellence. To discover the opportunities and find the community, we need to change the glasses we use to look at our work and workplace. If you view work through the shareholder-return lens, you will barely be able to pull yourself out of bed and into the office every day. Who wants to slave away to make wealthy people wealthier?

However, through the glasses marked "Excellence Every Day," you will discover that every task can be transformed from menial to an impact-making event that is easy to achieve. Better than that, you will suddenly see others around you in a new light, instantly recognizing those who *also* focus on excellence as a way of life. Sooner or later, if you continue to focus on excellence and work at it, you will find yourself part of a small community of "excellence believers." It is a matter of perspective. Either we succumb to the discouraging mission statement, or we create our own and build a strong group of people who make excellence their living mission statement.

Changing the glasses we use to view our daily challenges is not just a matter of switching a black lens to a pink lens. This is not an exercise in changing your attitude toward the same object and seeing the half-full vs. the half-empty glass. This is not a quest for changing the way we look at the world. It is much more real than that perspective change.

When we approach our work from the subjective perspective of the impact we make, our performance changes completely. When we are willing to take ownership of not only the task at hand but also the impact it has on others, we are at a completely different level of performance. By noticing the recipient of our work and focusing on delivering to that person (rather than to an abstract process target), we make a difference. By focusing our work efforts on the other person rather than on the process, we can strive to achieve excellence. The reason is quite simple: We can "do" excellence, when we want to do so. And when we see that we can make a real difference, we want to do excellence.

Mechanical Performance vs. Impact Performance

Every task and every job has mechanical elements or specific actions you must take to complete it. Your Daily Choice is about how you want to complete the task.

In some cases, there's also the option of delaying, deferring, or simply not completing the task. Unfortunately, this is an all-too-common affliction in mechanical work, hiding as it does behind the following rationalizations:

- "It's not my job."

- "I've done my part."

- "This is someone else's responsibility."

- "We're missing a form—we can't help until you've provided it."

- "The system does not allow me to do that."

- "You'll need to call another department."

- "These are the rules and I cannot change them."

- "I tried my best."

- "It requires approval from above."

- "I have no authority to do it."

- "It has never been done before."

These are just some of the excuses that accompany the side-stepping of a mechanical task. Whether we're making our customer jump through hoops or putting the burden (or blame) on another department or authority, our failure is in not taking ownership and committing to solve the problem. When we take this approach, we fail to recognize its impact on our customer, co-workers, and the organization.

Why when conducting mechanical tasks do we so frequently find ourselves shirking responsibility? Often, it's due to the mental and emotional exhaustion that comes with repetitious mechanical work; we can become frustrated and increasingly feel that we're not getting anywhere.

Well, it's no wonder we aren't getting anywhere if all we do is transfer responsibility to others all day, instead of taking ownership of anything. Acting like we are made of Teflon comes with a price: nothing sticks to us and therefore nothing gives us a sense of accomplishment. Sure, every task has boring elements to it. Expense reports drive me crazy, but I'm not going to let my work persona be defined based on this one unpleasant aspect of my job.

A hotel desk clerk takes specific actions to complete the check-in process. He greets the guest, uses the hotel's computer system to locate the original reservation, assigns a room, confirms the payment method, makes a magnetic key, creates a check-in folder that he hands to the guest, and points toward the elevators. In and of themselves, these actions are mundane, mechanical steps required to check in any new guest, and from that perspective, one might conclude that all guests are the same. This is the fast track to inertia and boredom. However, when the check-in is viewed from the guest's perspective, with thought given to the impact of the process on him, a unique experience unfolds with every new guest.

For the business traveler arriving at the hotel after taking the red-eye, noticing his tiredness is a basic courtesy, and the right room will make all the difference. Recognizing that we are helping a person to sleep, and thus to do his job better and ultimately to be more successful, transforms our work from routine mechanical to executive effective. For the couple checking in, marital stress may be the problem they are trying to solve, and the trip (including the hotel stay) may be a means of getting the marriage back on track. Treating them as just another reservation misses the entire point and does not make an impact. Trying to find them a pleasant room that provides the right ambience for them to rejuvenate their marriage and relieve their stress will make all the difference. This requires looking at the people standing before us and seeing them as people with unique needs. We can choose to focus on the impact that our performance will have on them, resisting the impulse to rush through the mechanical tasks involved in serving them.

The same thinking can be applied to virtually every task, from accounts payable and dealing with smaller suppliers who need help, to research jobs that have executive decisions dependent on the outcome, to IT work that can be viewed from the technology viewpoint or from the perspective of users who are not technology savvy. Every task has two sides to it: the mechanical side that focuses on process completion (irrespective of the recipient) and the impact side that focuses on the recipient's satisfaction and happiness.

The Daily Choice is about selecting the way we view our work: whether through the mundane, mechanical aspects of the task or through the impact on the recipient. By raising our heads out of our paperwork and looking at the person on the receiving end, we change the whole perspective of the value of our work. We can make it valuable by creating results that make a positive impact, or we may choose to ignore the person and create a negative impact instead. (Sometimes an individual's reaction to the person he is serving leads him to consciously create a negative impact as a form of revenge. People who make these types of choices have issues to address that are beyond the scope of this book.) Every work assignment or task has a person on the receiving end.

We just need to raise our eyes to look at this individual and then ask ourselves the following question.

"How Would I Want to Be Treated If I Were on the Receiving End?"

When you discover the obvious answer, your work will be shaped accordingly. You will not delegate responsibility to others like a seventh-degree Teflon master, but instead, you will solve the problem at hand and delight the recipient. By focusing on the other person, you naturally adapt your performance to deliver excellence. You will be associated with the impact made on someone else. Caring and passion—and therefore excellence—will become a natural part of your performance, because you *can* make a difference. By focusing on the other person, you are capable of fulfilling your childhood dreams of being a giving and contributing part of society and not simply parking on the receiving end. By focusing on the impact delivered by your performance, you can bring yourself to excellence naturally. You can make the choice to deliver superior performance. The Daily Choice is ultimately whether you focus your efforts on the mechanics of the task or on the impact on the individual. This is a choice of succumbing to the lowest, functional level of performance, or rising up to the highest level of making a difference.

In an article published by *USA Today* about the popular show *Extreme Makeover Home Edition*, the reporter noted that the production Web site receives more than 1,000 requests from volunteers every day. People from all walks of life throughout the country are willing to take time off from work and give up some income as a result, simply to help others. In the aftermaths of 9/11 and Hurricane Katrina, people left their workplaces in droves to volunteer and help survivors. Some did so for long periods of time at the risk of losing their jobs. Why would people be willing to risk their jobs to volunteer? The answer is simple: We humans possess a natural propensity to help our fellow beings, especially those in need.

Every day, we have a chance to make a difference. Every day, we can make our Daily Choice to deliver excellence to a fellow human being. We don't need a tragic disaster or a compelling TV show to let us discover the excellence capacity within us. We have the capacity to deliver excellence; it is our choice when and how we bring it to life. Every day, there are people who are direct recipients of our work. By focusing on the impact, we will deliver the type of performance worthy of a volunteer's commitment to develop a free operating system, rebuild someone's home, or comfort disaster victims.

When volunteering, we cope easily with both mundane work and hardships because we are so focused on the impact on others. The difficulties seem small and irrelevant to us. We can endure them for the sake of a higher purpose: making a difference in someone else's life, and ultimately making a contribution to the human community. This same principle can be applied to our livelihoods. Our daily work consists of many small, mundane actions that, when taken together, have a real impact on others. Adopting the same attitude in our everyday work that encourages us when volunteering will transform such ordinary tasks into extraordinary activities.

Inertia—Falling into a Performance Coma

We have all been there. We started a job all excited. We began learning new things, and we felt that we were growing. Then, seemingly without warning, inertia takes hold. Now, our work is more tiring and less exciting. It's become harder to get up in the morning. The passion is no longer there. What happened to all the exciting stuff? Where did all the challenges go? It seems as if we are just doing the same thing over and over again. The quality of our work seems to be slipping, too, but we're getting away with it so no big deal. We find ourselves easily irritated, and we can't wait for the weekend or our next day off.

For every person, inertia sinks in at a different time. It is usually a process, not an event. It does not happen overnight but happens so gradually that we don't really see it coming. Then, one day, we start feeling like a small screw in a large machine. Our sense of our value to the organization has diminished. We no longer feel we are contributing in a way that makes a difference. It looks like the company will be successful with or without us. If we were to take a six-month vacation, no one would notice.

Welcome to inertia.

How did it creep up on us? What happened to all those hopes and promises? Where did our excellence go?

Excellence did not disappear—we slipped.

We slipped from focusing on the person on the receiving end of our work and defaulted to the mechanics of the task. We stopped looking at the impact and shrank our focus to the functional elements of our work. We are performing with minimal accountability. We have slipped into a performance coma. We are working on autopilot, repeating old performances without attempting to create new excellence. We have become professional operators of processes rather than impact creators.

There are many factors that can lead to the slippage, and they'll be a little different for each of us. Perhaps you've seen your co-workers slacking off, not carrying their weight, not contributing to the overall work, while continually passing their responsibilities on to others. "Why should I try so hard or bother to care when nobody else does?" you may argue convincingly to yourself. Or, perhaps the workplace bureaucracy has worn you down, and you've decided that the owners or execs don't deserve your best. Instead, you'll punish them by withholding the excellence you're capable of doing. Perhaps your immediate supervisor has been treating you badly or with indifference. If that's the way he's going to be, you will no longer deliver your best to make him look good. After all, your performance reflects on him, and he doesn't deserve the credit. Another possibility is that you have simply grown weary in the absence of new challenges and a supportive work environment.

In all these cases, which are common for many people, slipping into inertia is a human reaction. It is natural to have these feelings; they are quite typical. However, in the process of reaching these conclusions and defaulting to rote mechanical performance, you have penalized yourself, first and foremost. By rejecting excellence and slipping into inertia, you have done yourself a disservice: You've given up the pleasure of delivering excellence, helping others, and being proud of the results of your work. You may have caused some damage to your employer or supervisor, but the damage to your personal well-being is certain to be much greater. Inertia silently forces you to make Daily Choices for the worst you can do and against excellence. It brings you to the mechanical performance level and wears you down. Ultimately, the cost to you is going to be greater than to anyone you may (consciously or not) intend to punish.

To fight inertia, you need to refocus your attention from the mechanics of the task to the impact your performance has on others. Focus on making a difference and having a positive impact on others. View your performance from that perspective. The relationships built through ongoing excellence performance delivered to others are often very fulfilling. Working with the same customers over a long period of time can allow you to see the cumulative impact of your work and gain further encouragement to continue to deliver excellence.

If you feel that you need a new challenge, or perhaps a new role, go ahead and pursue it. Do not stand still. If you let inertia rule, you will soon feel the void that comes from forgetting the recipient of your work and the impact you create. The results will include boredom, restlessness, the sense of a lack of fulfillment, and general dissatisfaction and unhappiness in your work. Your job will simply become one chore after another.

There is no standing still in excellence. If you do not choose to deliver excellence today, you are choosing mediocrity. If you are not rowing your boat toward excellence today, it does not sit still; it is drawn to the familiar current of routine mechanical performance. Every day, each choice is a choice *for* or *against* excellence, but not a choice for status quo. Do not let inertia fool you. Make a choice and change your environment, if you think it will help, and avoid the trap of expecting things to get better without any effort. If you slipped, admit it, and make the choice to go back to excellence. Stop blaming the world and *create* the world that can support your pursuit of excellence.

Make It Personal

In certain professions, it is difficult to relate to the innermost feelings of the "customer." If you are a cardiologist, for instance, you can never fully understand what patients are going through until and unless you've had a heart attack. You may have an excellent grasp of a patient's medical condition, but relating to her deepest emotions is another matter. Similarly, a firefighter will find it difficult to truly appreciate the sense of loss felt by those he serves unless a fire has ravaged his own home, allowing him to experience firsthand what it's like to lose every worldly belonging and find oneself suddenly homeless. Of course, we're not all doctors and emergency workers, and in many other professions, understanding the customer should be much easier due to our shared common ground.

In the working world, someone is on the receiving end of every effort, living with the consequences of the work's quality. When the work is great, the recipient is delighted; when it's mediocre, the recipient suffers. We ourselves are continually on the receiving end of the work of others. When we wake up in the morning and brush our teeth, we are customers of the toothpaste manufacturer. When we eat breakfast, we are customers of the cereal manufacturer. While driving to work, we are customers of the automobile manufacturers or the transit service. We know very well what it means to be a customer and what type of quality and service level a customer reasonably demands and expects. We know it very well.

So, we are all customers. Yet, somehow, as we enter our workplaces or as we punch in or swipe our ID cards and rush to our stations, a transformation occurs: We mysteriously transform from customers to managers. We shed the customer perspective gained in our personal lives and start behaving like managers of a faceless company that takes its customers for granted. We treat others in ways we would never accept if we were the customers. We make decisions and take actions that the customer side of us would find offensive and unacceptable. As customers, we do not understand the logic of such decisions, but as managers, we feel obliged to make them.

"It's not personal, just business," the cliché goes. But excellence is not just business. Excellence is personal. Delivering excellence comes not from paychecks, but from a personal wish to be the best through doing the best. It is only when we take our work and the outcome of our actions personally that we can start delivering excellence. If it is not personal, it will never be excellence. When it is not personal, it is devoid of passion, creativity, and innovation. When we call it "business," we create an excuse to not make it personal and, therefore, we fail to deliver excellence. We try to disguise ourselves and not assume responsibility. When we make it all business, we do not care; we just go through the motions and deliver an unacceptable level of performance—unacceptable by customers, just like us.

We should not forget the unique training that we've undergone as customers: It has prepared us to fully appreciate the expectations of the person on the receiving end of our work, be it an external or an internal customer. We are aware when mechanical performance has let us down, and we know when performance reaches the level of excellence. We are best able to deliver excellence when we relate both to the customer within us who knows what excellence is and to the customer we are actually serving. By making it personal, we can make it excellence.

Hey, You! Yes, You!

Catherine "Kitty" Genovese was walking in New York City one day in 1964 when she was attacked by a serial rapist and murdered. The 19-year-old was stabbed multiple times by the attacker and left to die a slow painful death. In fact, Kitty was left bleeding in the street for 30 minutes before she actually died. In that span of time, 38 witnesses saw Kitty and heard her cry for help. But none chose to call the police or otherwise lend a hand and help save her life.

The inertia of the many witnesses in this case was described variously as the bystander effect, bystander apathy, or the diffusion of responsibility; ultimately, it became known as the Kitty Genovese Syndrome. The bystander effect represents a physiological phenomenon in which individuals who witness an emergency situation will fail to intervene and help the victim while others are present. Following the Kitty Genovese case, similar cases in which bystanders failed to assist in emergency situations were recorded and publicized.

In 1968, John Darley and Bibb Latane tested the bystander effect in a lab and concluded that the lack of assistance is not a product of carelessness. In fact, bystanders who were alone at a scene were more likely to help then those who were in the presence of others. The reason for the lack of intervention is attributed to the belief that others are more qualified to do the job and the belief that someone else will intervene and save the day. In my experience, unfortunately, this "diffusion of responsibility" is a common phenomenon that is not limited to life and death situations. Gradually, we diffuse or delegate more and more opportunities for excellence to others as we assume less and less responsibility personally. Somehow we become humble, deciding we can trust others' ability to perform more than our own. Excuse me if I do not buy this newly discovered humility. It sounds more like an excuse not to take responsibility than a genuine trust in the capabilities of others. To avoid responsibility and action, it appears we are prepared to trust almost *anyone* and to believe that virtually *everyone* is more capable than we are.

Of course, in delivering excellence, this approach is counterproductive. Delivering excellence requires the direct opposite of the bystander effect. The idea here is that there is no person more qualified to do the job than you. You are it. Regardless of who else is out there, when it's time to act decisively, it is *not* the time for humility (express your humility later, when you get all the raves). If we are committed to excellence, we need to recognize the bystander effect and disarm its debilitating impact by taking action. Avoid surveying the people around you and simply do it. Kitty's tragic story should serve as a guiding light for us to assume responsibility as soon as we see a need. We can use the lesson of her death to save others.

Excellence is not the province of bystanders. Excellence is about taking action and making things happen. We are not observers, but rather creators. We owe it to those in need, and to ourselves, to recognize our abilities as the best available in any given situation.

Be Proud of Your Masterpiece

When walking on San Francisco's famous Fisherman's Wharf, you will encounter many sidewalk artists ready to paint. They are equipped with small tables, watercolor paint and brushes, and samples of their work. These artists are expert in painting names in the Asian style, decorated with leaping dolphins and palm trees. For a mere $5, customers can choose their preferred color and decorative style, and within minutes, the artist will complete and sign their newest masterpiece.

Just across the street from these artists, you'll find a variety of high-end galleries selling the works of other talented painters for $5,000 or more per canvas. While thinking about both types of artists, I started to wonder how it is that one works in the cold to earn $5 a painting while the other makes a thousand times that amount working in a heated studio.

There are many differences between the street artists and the gallery artists, of course. Some will argue that the amount of time it takes to create a gallery work justifies the price difference. I think there is a more meaningful and fundamental difference that involves the artistic process. The street artists are simply doing mechanical work, following the precise instructions given by the customer without bringing any passion to the effort. They are not attempting to create masterpieces; it's just work and a way to make a living. For these street painters, expert as they are in the mechanical task of painting, art is no more than a production line process.

On the other hand, the so-called fine artists whose paintings hang in the gallery take tremendous pride in their work. They paint with passion and love. It's not just work for them; it's personal. They make a special effort to create excellence. They may use similar brushes, tools, and colors, and go through similar motions to those of the street artists, but they add special ingredients—creativity, vision, passion, and pride—and it shows. These artists are expert in the passion of painting.

The pricing of these two distinct types of art—both of which are valid, of course—reflects the difference between the impassioned effort of the gallery artist and the mechanical expertise of the street artist. Their respective customers understand the difference and reward each artist accordingly.

When you review the results of your work every day, would you frame them and hang them on the wall? Are you creating masterpieces or street paintings? The key to excellence is to create masterpieces. You can't do that by going through the motions, but only from a personal place where you are deeply committed to the outcome. The essence of the Daily Choice is to determine whether you want to deliver a street painting or a work of art. Do you want to create something exceptional, or just get it done? When considering your Daily Choice, ask yourself: Would I sign this and hang it on the wall? Would I include it as a highlight of my resume? Would I share the story of how I did it for the sake of posterity?

It Is All Around Us

The opportunities for excellence are all around us. They come in many different forms: emails requesting help, demands for an unexpected report, a fellow employee facing a problem with new software, a customer calling with a billing problem, a guest showing up early and in desperate need of a room, a new deadline for a proposal, a leaking faucet, a hysterical patient in need of medical help, or a lost person seeking directions. All around us are people who need and seek our help. They are a burden if we choose to see them as such; alternatively, they are also opportunities to create masterpieces. It is up to us to choose how to view and to respond to them.

We do not need to wait for tragic events, once-in-a-lifetime opportunities, or legendary occurrences. Every new day brings opportunities to transform tedious mechanical work to fine art in a moment of Daily Choice. Rather than planning to do excellence one day in the future, or waiting for opportunity to knock on the door, we need to discover excellence in everything we do. The opportunities are as numerous as the people we meet and communicate with every day. The people who are impacted by the results of our work *are* our opportunities for excellence. We just need to raise our heads from the mechanical work to see them. We need to take our minds off the addictive, cynical jokes that reinforce our attitude of inaptitude and commit to perform at our highest level. We must stop citing all the reasons we can't and start making things happen. We cannot expect to deliver excellence without obstacles. Obstacles will always be part of the challenge of excellence. We can choose to ascend to excellence by facing the obstacles head on, or descend to mediocrity using the obstacles as excuses.

In preparing to write this book, I undertook a search for stories that bring the commitment to and delivery of excellence performance to life. I used certain criteria for the excellence stories and practices I elected to include. Since the premise of the book is that excellence is not the realm of the few, the rare, and the legendary, but rather that there is an excellence capacity within each of us, my focus was on presenting stories and practices that would inspire readers and that they could emulate. I was searching for stories of everyday heroes that anyone can relate to, stories that support the case for excellence every day and everywhere. And because I believe that genuine willingness is all that's necessary to make an impact, I looked for examples of efforts that succeeded without any special skills or budgets.

I wanted stories demonstrating a "Wow!" factor, so that readers might visualize the astonished looks on the faces of customers saying, "What a surprise—I did not expect *that!*" Excellence in a vacuum is a self-serving exercise, and I do not believe it can truly be achieved without making a difference in someone's life—even if it's just bringing a smile to a person's face. Giving to others and delighting employees and customers through amazing performance is the pinnacle of excellence.

A simple Daily Choice for excellence by someone like you is all it takes to make it happen. I hope the stories that follow inspire you to make the Daily Choice and fulfill your capacity to deliver the type of performance that really makes a difference. If you read these stories and say, "I can do that," then I've achieved my goal. Go to my Web site and let me know, and, while you're at it, please share a story of your own— many other readers are sure to read and appreciate it, and so will I.

CHAPTER 9

Excellence Daily Choice— Personal Leadership

Performance at the Moment of Truth

Do you remember the thrill the first time you went to see a car race? Few people are immune to that kind of excitement. The amazing speed of the cars, the roar of the engines, the pressure of winning, the competition between the drivers—these are some of the signature aspects of a thrilling car race.

At the races, the drivers are considered the stars, and they get all the limelight. What they do is risky, and the stakes are high, making the race even more exciting for those of us in the stands. However, there are other top racetrack performers whose roles are equally impressive. Unlike the drivers, these individuals are rarely acknowledged; the TV cameras ignore them, focusing instead on the track. Nevertheless, their work is critical to the driver's ability to perform and (potentially) to win the race. While the driver's excellence is judged by how fast he drives, theirs is judged by how they fast they can service the car and get it back into the race.

During a Formula 1 race in Europe, I had the opportunity to witness a special excellence performance. I was watching the race from the Paddock Club, from a vantage point above the pit that allowed me to view all the activities of the cars and drivers. While I had seen auto racing on TV, this in-person experience was much more intense. I found many things about the race intriguing but one particular aspect caught my attention above all else.

Seven seconds was all it took and then the car was gone. During this time, 25 mechanics had successfully lifted the car with jacks, replaced all four tires, refueled the gas tank, and reconnected and updated the electronics systems. Surprisingly, this feat is by no means unique: Seven seconds is the average length of time for a Formula 1 pit stop. To achieve Swiss-like precision, the mechanics go through years of intensive training. These highly skilled mechanics can replace a tire in three seconds (three mechanics are assigned to one tire), and in less than eight-tenths of a second, they can get a nozzle connected and begin refueling the vehicle. The story of a pit stop and those who get the job done is inspiring: It takes precision, commitment, the ability to work under intense pressure, and, ultimately, a desire to win. Pit stop mechanics don't bask in the limelight, but they are excellence performers who are critical to the outcome of every race.

Can you imagine what would happen if a mechanic stopped to consult his manager during a pit stop? In the time it took to raise his hand, the race would be lost. As I observed the pit crew at my race, I recognized that in their unified and flawless performance, there was no room for politics, complaints, or any appeals to the boss. Each mechanic was intensely focused on completing his task perfectly, minimizing errors and time delays while ensuring the safety of the car and its driver.

In the pit, a simple mistake or delay can cost the race, and in worst cases, it could cost the driver his life. In an environment where every second counts, a pit stop is completed in an average of seven seconds; a shorter pit stop, during which the crew only fills half the tank, may take a mere 4.5 seconds. In both cases, before you know it, the car is back in the race. Excellence is measured in seconds; no team can afford even a second's delay. Everyone works together to complete their tasks as efficiently as possible in an exquisitely choreographed performance under the command of the lollipop man (the chief mechanic who holds the stop sign, or "lollipop," and controls the pit stop performance). Using an open intercom system, he provides any special or emergency directions to a few key mechanics and ensures that his team performs in perfect concert.

"People think the pit stop is a game," says Sam Michael, technical director of the Williams F1 team, "but it is, in fact, very dangerous. The risk associated with working the pit stop is quite high and only the rare and few will qualify." He adds, "I've been an engineer for 12 years and I will not perform a pit stop." Given the danger and risk inherent in this type of work, pit stop performance is judged not only from the perspective of speed and precision but by the level of attention to safety issues.

When mechanics perform at such a high level, they can achieve seemingly miraculous results. Early on in the race, a Mercedes McLaren was pulled in three times with mechanical problems. Such stops can cost the driver a significant amount of time and hurt his position in the race. Amazingly, as the result of successful teamwork in the pit, the delays were held to a minimum, and the Mercedes won the race. Such an impressive accomplishment must be attributed not only to the skill of the driver but to the team whose flawless performance during those three critical pit stops kept the car in the race. Their commitment to excellence, in spite of serious mechanical challenges, resulted in victory against all odds.

Excelling in pit stop conditions requires a team that is physically fit with a calm and focused attitude. Strong coordination skills are needed along with a relentless drive to perfect the performance and shave off an additional second every time. In our daily lives, we hardly notice when two seconds have gone by, but in the pit, those same two seconds can make the difference between winning and losing.

So what was it about this pit stop that made such a tremendous impression on me? First, there was the amazing teamwork among the 25 people working under such tremendous pressure. Their intense focus on the job at hand—their ability to ignore any and all potential distractions—was a critical component of their excellence. I was equally impressed by the lack of conflict, cynicism, or finger-pointing that is so common in stressful situations involving teams of co-workers. Apparently, seven seconds leaves no time for this type of thing. Everyone was intensely focused on his task, knowing full well that even the slightest mistake would carry a devastating price. Each of them bore responsibilities with pride and responded to them with excellence performance.

That brings us to the concept of empowerment. In the pit, the mechanics make the split-second decisions. Each of them is empowered to do what he believes must be done without management approval. The pit crew simply cannot afford to work under other conditions. When replacing a tire, a mechanic might notice a defective disk that could damage the braking system and pose a safety risk to the driver. It's his job to assess and fix the problem without delay.

As I watched one particularly dramatic pit stop crew in action, a jack collapsed, pinning a mechanic beneath the front of the car. In a matter of seconds, five of his peers lifted the car, pulled him out, removed the broken jack, and still managed to keep the stop under 10 seconds. No questions asked.

These mechanics use the information that's in front of them; they are trained to make on-the-spot decisions with full confidence and management backing. Each is fully empowered to do his job and recognizes the implications of a split-second delay or a bad decision. When your performance is measured in seven-second intervals, you better know what you are doing. You better focus on excellence. And most of all, you better forget your boss. There's no time to ask for permission, to delegate to someone else, or to find a scapegoat for your decision. This is you, at the moment of truth, facing another Daily Choice.

Excellence is the ability to make decisions at such moments of truth. These decisions are the essence of "response-ability" (a topic we covered in some depth in Chapter 4). Your ability to respond to challenges is directly linked to your ability to make decisions and solve the challenge at hand.

At Williams F1, team decisions are fully delegated, in terms of both authority and responsibility, to the mechanics in the pit—the individuals who have the most information and who see a problem with their own eyes. During my race, I was impressed to see a number of cars pulled out of the competition due to an engineer's decision. Engineers, unlike mechanics, are not involved in the pit stop; during the race, their job is to assess vehicle performance continuously and ensure safety via hundreds of sensors communicating real-time data wirelessly to control computers. Based on this information, an engineer is empowered to pull "his" cars from the race. The driver—who may be a top star earning millions of dollars annually—has no say: The engineer's decision goes. Why? Because at the moment of truth, it is the engineer who has the information necessary to make a good decision. Neither earning power nor established hierarchy have anything to do with making the right decision. The key is possessing relevant information along with the experience and judgment to interpret it correctly.

As a leader, the true test is allowing people who actually face the problem at hand to make decisions. On paper, every executive swears that employees are empowered to make such decisions; however, when the moment of truth arrives, many employees default to the boss to actually make the decision. Unlike the Formula 1 mechanics and engineers, these employees avoid the risk of making a critical decision. Why is that?

There are a number of reasons employees may fail to make decisions at the moment of truth, including:

1. We fail to see the moment of truth – Employees may believe that the customer is prepared to wait for them and, therefore, fail to deliver the desired result immediately. Without a sense of urgency, it's easy to miss the narrow window of opportunity for delivering exceptional results.

2. Lack of information – Employees may not have the information necessary to make decisions at the moment of truth. Such a lack of information impairs their ability to make good, confident decisions.

3. Lack of authority – The empowerment of employees is a threat for many managers: If employees are able to make the critical decisions, the manager believes he may be viewed as irrelevant. Although managers won't admit to this fear, they demonstrate it through their actions.

4. Lack of permission to fail – When employees are afraid of being punished for making wrong decisions, they will simply avoid making difficult decisions. Only in environments

where employees are allowed to fail will they dare to make the types of difficult decisions that lead to excellence.

5. Lack of motivation – Experience tells us there is a certain percentage of employees who simply seek a paycheck, not greater responsibility or work they truly care about. These employees simply do not want the extra pressure and accountability that comes with decision-making.

6. Lack of experience – You can't make good split-second decisions without experience. Without experience, and the confidence and intuition that experience brings, employees will hesitate to make those difficult decisions.

In order to achieve an organizationwide capability to perform and make decisions at the moment of truth, employees first need to feel confident that management will be there to support them when they try and fall short.

The true test of resilience and competitiveness is your ability to make decisions at the moment of truth. What decisions can you make in seven seconds? What decisions can your employees make in less than seven seconds? What excellence can they deliver in seven seconds? Customers test their suppliers at moments of truth. The impatient ones don't have time to wait for escalations, transfers, referrals, and management decisions. In today's competitive business environment, an employee needs to do more than simply record and report a complaint. She must act fast to resolve the problem before the moment of truth is lost, and with it, the opportunity for excellence.

"Good mechanics are constantly perfecting the pit stop," according to F1's Sam Michael. "These mechanics carry the entire company on their shoulders. A mistake can lose the whole Grand Prix and create a high risk." He adds, "It takes a very special person." These special people can perform during a moment of truth and very often determine the fate of a driver and the outcome of a race.

If you were to ask a Formula 1 race engineer or mechanic, "How did you make that decision?" He would most likely respond with: "It was the obvious decision." With years of training and experience, decisions come naturally and excellence becomes a habit for these men and women. The Daily Choice becomes second nature. They act on the information available to them, relying on well-honed instincts and highly specialized knowledge to do the right thing at the moment of truth every day. They know that a split-second's hesitation can mean losing the race, or—in the worst case—even the driver's life.

In aspiring to and achieving this level of conviction, we, too, will deliver excellence every day.

In Search of the Right Customer

The search for customers is an eternal pursuit for all companies. In their zeal to increase market share, executives spend good money on marketing programs and slick salespeople to attract as many customers as possible. But could we be attracting the *wrong* customers? Is there even such a thing as a *wrong* customer?

Yes, absolutely! Customers who are a mismatch to your value proposition will tend to become argumentative, abusive, high maintenance, and, overall, unprofitable. The situation presents a tough choice: Do you work to keep such customers because you fear losing them to a competitor, or do you cut the cord and send them on their way?

In my book, the choice comes down to succumbing to mediocrity while serving the wrong customers or delivering excellence to the right customers. The quest for market share can come at the expense of profitability, and when working with the wrong customers, it's a trade-off that most executives fail to see or choose to ignore. They want to believe they can chase the last dollar and keep the business profitable. In reality, by over-serving customers who will never return a profit, they misallocate resources and fail to delight profitable (aka, the right) customers.

A few executives share a secret regarding the pursuit of customers. These rare executives know that not all customers are worth pursuing; they know that some will never return a profit. And when you work with the wrong customers, there is simply no way to deliver excellence, every day or *any* day. The wrong customers will not recognize or appreciate the value delivered to them. To deliver excellence every day, you must focus on the right customers.

For executives who know the secret, "firing" the wrong customers is the essence of a win–win situation. By letting these unprofitable customers go to competitors, they win twice. Their competitors are now busy dealing with the wrong customers, while they are creating excellence for the right ones.

It takes courage for an executive to let go of the wrong customers (after all, we paid good money to bring them in). Anne Csuka, vice president of operations for CATIC, a New England-based title insurance underwriter, is this type of executive. Not only does Anne know the secret that not all customers are good customers, but she has the courage to be selective about which customers to keep. As a company, CATIC now fires the wrong customers, a process that Anne put into motion by first developing profiles of the "wrong" customers, based on each customer's level of business with the company, the number of complaints, their overall usage of the company's time and resources, and even factors such as the language customers use when speaking with employees.

"There comes a point when you simply realize that you cannot be the best for everyone," Anne says. "Customers are so different, and your excellence can fit the needs of some, but not all. It takes two for excellence performance, and if one side is not ready or willing, nothing our employees do will help. We need to make sure we have the right customers, the ones who are ready and willing." She adds, "You need to focus on those who appreciate your excellence."

Using its profile system, CATIC identifies specific customers who meet the undesirable criteria and offers them a choice: either change their behavior or stop using the free services the company provides.

It takes guts to approach a customer this way and to willingly let them go to competitors. It presents a mental obstacle that most executives cannot overcome and, as a result, the company continues to throw good money after bad. It's a shame because this is precisely the type of leadership excellence that sends a strong message to employees. When employees see executives weeding out the wrong customers—especially the abusive ones—they quickly realize that management is serious about creating an optimal environment that delivers excellence rather than creating impossible situations for them.

Not surprisingly, the initial response from customers to Anne's effort was mixed. Some customers could not have cared less and left—a pure savings for the company since it had no further need to invest in them. These clients were clearly a mismatch. Other customers recognized the value CATIC had already delivered to them and agreed to adhere to the new terms to stay on board. Both responses were welcomed by Anne. The customers who left freed up resources that the firm was able to refocus on the right customers, while the customers who stayed have come to benefit more fully from CATIC's services and even appreciate them. According to Anne, the positive impacts have included improved employee morale and motivation, an increased emphasis on delighting customers, and greater profitability.

"The customers were pretty shocked when we approached them with our message," she reports. "They did not believe we would actually stick to our plan. But we did and the smart customers made the choice to stay with us and be good customers."

Anne's actions were remarkable not only in her willingness to create the right environment to excel, but by her assumption of execution responsibility. Executives too often delegate the unpleasant work to underlings, yet Anne did the initial outreach before asking anyone else to get involved. The message she sent to the rest of the organization was clear: Working with the right customers rather than wasting resources on the wrong ones is a top priority worthy of her time—and, thus, worthy of any other employee's time. This executive behavior showcased the importance of excellence and a commitment to maintaining and nurturing an environment that supports excellence performance.

Focusing on the right customers is essential if you are going to deliver excellence. A relationship that is mismatched will lead to wasted efforts and neglect of the right customers. Pursuing the right customers and weeding out the rest does not require the allocation of tremendous resources or a sizable investment in strategic planning. It is as simple as picking up the phone, calling your "wrong customers," and discussing the matter. This is the kind of excellence that can be done every day by anyone, but it takes courage—the kind of courage Anne demonstrated to her employees.

Do you have the courage to let the wrong customers go? (For that matter, do you even know who are they?) How will *not* letting these customers go impact your ability to excel? Excellence requires two: you and the recipient. If you want excellence to thrive, follow Anne's example and focus on the right recipients.

To Tie or Not to Tie: That Is Not the Question

When a new CEO arrived at one of the Siemens companies, he brought with him a new culture. He wore a suit and tie every day; meanwhile, everyone else dressed business casual. Soon, rumors started about the company's dress code, and employees approached their managers for clarification. Some managers replied quickly, instructing their employees to switch to the "new" dress code and dress more formally at work. But not Joe Accardi.

When Joe's people approached him about how they should dress, he refused to provide instructions and instead told his people to make their own decisions. His approach was met with some frustration, and in rare cases, even anger. "Why can't you just tell us what to do?" some employees demanded. After all, other managers were providing clear directions to the question of "To tie or not to tie?" However, Joe understood what many other managers failed to grasp. If you keep making these types of decisions for employees, it eventually begins to strip away ownership of and responsibility for their own actions. It can be tempting for a manager to make all the decisions, even gratifying, but the gratification is not worth the high cost of working with employees who will not take responsibility. If they will not make decisions, they will not take responsibility for their actions. And performing actions without responsibility can only lead to mediocrity.

Joe's position was, "I refuse to make the decision whether or not to wear a tie. It's your decision, not mine." He told me, "In the end, it is far more important to live by the principle of empowerment than to have people wear ties. I need my people to own their choices because it is the only way they will do it well." Joe recognizes that when employees get orders or instructions from above, they execute them reluctantly. When they make their own decisions, they do so with pride. Excellence can result when people make their own choices. Because he understands that fine distinction, Joe wants to let his people take ownership of the decision, and ultimately, over their excellence.

In this case, Joe did not succumb to pressure; each employee had to make his own decision. It was a small victory on the path to much larger victories.

The question of responsibility often starts with small questions such as "To tie or not to tie?" The temptation is hard to resist for managers who want to get it over with and make the decision. But succumbing to such temptation will bear longer-term consequences. If your employees struggle with basic questions such as how to dress for work, they are not ready to deliver excellence. Whether due to a lack of willingness or ability, they are missing the whole excellence commitment. It starts with small decisions and leads to bigger ones. It starts with small risks and leads to taking bigger ones. For Joe, it was never a question of "to tie or not to tie." It was a question of people's responsibility and accountability. To achieve that, Joe knew he must withdraw a bit and provide his people with enough space to own their decisions and actions.

The road to excellence is a journey taken one decision at a time.

CHAPTER 10

Excellence
Daily Choice—
Taking Ownership

Waiting at the Altar

Standing at the altar can be a moment of truth—there is definitely a decision to be made there. But for Barbara Boegner and Gustav Myburgh, the day they were to meet at the altar presented a different type of a critical choice. Like most people, they had prepared for the wedding day diligently. They had a vivid picture of a beautiful wedding with all their loved ones gathered in the church to join them for this important moment in their lives. As the couple was on the way to the chapel, they noticed an incident on the road. Friends and family were already gathered in the church waiting for the bride and groom to arrive, but the couple was not on time. With no real explanation for the delay, the guests waited patiently for more than 45 minutes until the bride and groom finally arrived to tie the knot.

The reason for the delay was not a traffic jam. From the car, the couple had seen three armed men holding a driver at gunpoint in the middle of the road. Most people facing such a situation would have naturally run in the other direction. With the bride-to-be dressed in her white gown and the prospective groom in his smart suit, they had a tough choice to make. With hundreds of guests waiting for them, it might have seemed like an easy decision. After all, your wedding is a pretty strong excuse. But they made a different choice: They decided to confront the hijackers, and when they did, the hijackers jumped into a truck and fled. At this point, the choice became tougher—to chase or not to chase, with hundreds of people still waiting at the chapel. But for Barbara and Gustav, the choice was simple and rather obvious. They did not think twice before chasing the hijackers, then catching and arresting the gunmen.

But there is one important fact: Both are law enforcement officers in the Johannesburg police. They face hijackers and criminals every day, and when they had to choose between continuing to the church and getting married or dealing with the gunmen, their personal allegiance to their duty guided their split-second decision under these difficult circumstances. By making this type of choice, it is obvious that being law enforcement officers was not a job for them, but rather, it was a personal mission. This personal mission made them pursue the hijackers, even at the great expense of delaying their wedding plans. In a sense, their intuition guided them. They made the Daily Choice for excellence even when they were not officially on the job. As their story illustrates, the commitment to excellence and the focus on the impact transcends rules and procedures.

Barbara and Gustav represent a different type of employee—those who come to work to fulfill a personal mission. They relate to their work as if it is a personal calling. They derive personal meaning and fulfillment from their work, not merely a salary. They do not go to work reluctantly, because it is the only way they can find to make money. Monetary compensation is one dimension of their work, but it is not the only or primary one. The Johannesburg police are blessed to have Barbara and Gustav among their law enforcement officers.

What would your employees do in such a situation? When faced with stressful, time-sensitive decisions, would your employees follow the impact on others or personal satisfaction? Do your employees limit their job commitment to working hours? The answers to these questions offer a pretty clear indication of your organization's willingness to commit to excellence.

If you need time to think about these questions, the answer is clear. When your employees are willing to delay their wedding and keep all the guests waiting at the chapel until they get the job done, you know you have arrived. I know that it sounds a bit extreme, but only if you do not believe in the cause. Barbara and Gustav do not see police work as a 9-to-5 paycheck; they see it as a mission that does not stop at the end of a shift. It was a mission that was calling them even when they were dressed for their wedding, ready to tie the knot. They internalized the mission, and the importance and impact it had on others. As such, when the Daily Choice presented itself (and sometimes it is on "The Day"), they chose excellence without thinking twice. It came natural to them because of their commitment to excellence and probably multiple Daily Choices they made before that day. The sum of all these choices put them on the path of excellence as a natural reaction when the opportunity presented itself. What a great way to add meaning to a personal relationship by sharing values and making them a reality. Not exactly the wedding day most people plan, but then, things don't always go according to plan. They are proof that excellence opportunities present themselves every day, even on "The Day."

Chocolate Chips to the Rescue!

I was shopping at Wal-Mart (Store 2049, Altoona, PA) on Tuesday, September 16. After arriving home, I discovered I had left my purse in a cart outside Wal-Mart.

My daughter and I immediately went back to Wal-Mart, but the cart was not there. We went to the courtesy desk, where my purse was returned by Regina Murphy and Terri Stehley, who found it after looking through many carts. All my papers and credit cards were inside, but all the cash was missing.

The following Sunday, I received a call to come to Wal-Mart. To my surprise, Regina and Terri gave me an envelope filled with cash in the amount I lost. They had baked chocolate chip cookies and held a bake sale for employees so they could return my money!

Terri (domestic department) and Regina (housewares department) deserve the highest award Wal-Mart can give. I also want to recognize Manager Sam Gortney and all the employees of the Altoona Wal-Mart. I am deeply grateful to all at that store.

Thank you,
Helen L. Mauro
Hollidaysburg, PA

I was personally inspired by this story, which appeared in the 1998 Wal-Mart annual report. Since then, I have shared it with thousands of people through my seminars. The personal ownership that Terri and Regina took in this situation was impressive. It was not their fault. They finished their shift and should have gone home. They could have easily dismissed it as Wal-Mart's problem. After all, Wal-Mart is a wealthy company with plenty of resources, and if Wal-Mart wanted to delight its customers, it could easily afford to compensate Helen. Regina and Terri could have dismissed it with excuses; they certainly had plenty of very good ones at their disposal.

But they chose a different path. They did not let any arguments excuse them from the path to excellence. Neither Terri nor Regina viewed their work as a mechanical task, but instead, they took personal pride in serving customers at their Wal-Mart store. If someone steals or hurts another customer at *their* Wal-Mart store, then it is personal. They relate to their work as a mission to help people, and they view it from the total impact the situation makes on people. In this context, their Daily Choice was obvious. They had to do something to rectify the negative impact endured by Helen at their Wal-Mart store. They were not out to fix all the problems at all the Wal-Marts or stop global thievery forever. They simply wanted to make Helen happier.

That is the essence of excellence every day by every person. It is a personal commitment to superior performance. It is the commitment to make a positive impact on others. Such superior performance is a result of a choice to make excellence a personal standard. It doesn't come from allowing the counter-arguments—as logical as they might be—to distract you from reaching to a higher standard of performance. If you think that delivering excellence is difficult, ask yourself a simple question: How many chocolate chip cookies have you baked for your customers today? The answer is simple if you take personal pride and ownership in the impact it makes on others.

Never Give Up

This is the story of Gena who works at New Jersey–based Alpine limousine service.

We were starting a typical workday when the first plane hit the tower. One of our longtime broadcasting clients was instantly sent on assignment to cover the World Trade Center, and we obliged as usual by providing a driver right away. Minutes later, when the second tower was hit, an immediate concern was Rockefeller Center. I feared it would also be targeted because the world knows that NBC airs its news from that building.

I tried phoning my client, which only increased my fears: None of the many phone numbers on file were responding. I tried many different departments, to no avail, but I didn't want to give up. Luckily, she called me back, giving me a sense of relief—relief that was short-lived as the client stated clearly, "I am taking your driver." I began shaking, watching this situation unfold before my eyes on the news. The client couldn't possibly be aware of the danger that was evident from my perspective. I cautioned the driver, "Don't take her too close! The building is on fire, so try to have enough room to drive out of there should the worst happen."

Little did I know the worst would follow shortly. With great persistence, I continued to try to contact my client's senior staff and control room with no luck. I told the driver, "Don't leave your customer on her own, stay and wait for her!" My driver's cell phone went dead, which was heart-stopping. Luckily, though, the two-way radio still worked, and we were able to stay in touch.

I insisted that our driver not leave the passenger behind; my persistence would not allow me to let go of the driver *or* the passenger. Every second felt like a lifetime. I reminded the driver to keep talking, so that I would know he was OK. Then it happened: The building began collapsing and I could no longer reach driver or passenger. At that moment, I felt as if I had failed both of them. Why did I allow my driver to get so close to the towers? Our radios went silent for a long time, shortly after, the towers collapsed.

I began frantically sending text messages. After two harrowing hours—maybe more—my driver phoned our 800 number. I couldn't believe my ears: The passenger made it out alive. If not for the "never-give-up" spirit, something I constantly preach to my team, I would have lost a driver and a client.

It was a time I will never forget. Because dedication is something I strongly embrace, I dedicate my life to my job. I don't give my job 80%, but 120%. I strive to help young operators with little life experience, hoping to give them the opportunity to grow, mature and learn about being dedicated, not only to themselves and to our company, but also—and most importantly—to our clients.

Gena allows her customer to define her success. The company serves NBC as well as several other media companies and defines success through tight deadlines and a few crazy requests from customers to do their jobs well. If her customers want to push the envelope, Gena is there to help them out. There were many reasons not to send this driver, nor to allow this customer to pursue such a dangerous situation, but Gena made it happen. It takes a willingness to take risks to create excellence.

The easy way out would have been to give up and say no at the outset. The excellence way is to stay connected until all involved are safe and the mission is accomplished. Giving up and saying no are the easy way out for any difficult Daily Choice. They often seem like the safest choice, but the truth is less intuitive: Not taking risks is the greatest risk of all. Not choosing excellence is never safe. It is dangerous because we send customers to the hands of competitors. Not choosing excellence is never an option for Gena. She is now committed to transfering this knowledge and experience to others at Alpine Limousine, so that they also will all define success from their customers' perspectives.

Sharing her experience with others takes Gena's commitment to excellence to new heights. Not only does she care about her own standards, but she is also concerned about the excellence of those around her. She knows that making courageous decisions to perform excellence requires knowledge and expertise, and she is committed to sharing those with others to help them make similar excellence decisions. To whom did you teach excellence today?

In Sickness and in Health

The following story was submitted by my good friend, David Cohen, the general manager of the David InterContinental Hotel in Tel Aviv, Israel. David's commitment to excellence is legendary, and his employees live those values every day. As a recipient of their service, I am a witness to the honesty and caring that they bring to every interaction with every guest.

No one likes to get sick far away from home. It is probably one of the worst experiences a traveler can have. But at the David InterContinental, being sick away from home can actually be a pleasant experience (or at least not a bad one). I decided to keep this story in its original form as it was submitted and let it speak for itself.

> However much you prepare for any circumstance, no matter how much you brief your staff and set procedures, sooner or later the unexpected is bound to happen.
>
> This is the story of a guest in trouble, whose bad experience is turned into a good memory of human warmth and friendship.
>
> It all started as a normal shift until …

I received an alarming call from an elderly lady in the hotel at 10 AM. I could hear that she had great difficulty in breathing and was in a state of panic. I immediately put everything I was doing aside in order to take charge of the situation. She had had an unfortunate accident in her hotel room, and, after assessing the situation, I decided to take her to the nearest hospital.

Even though she was now in the capable hands of the medical staff at the hospital, I felt that as a guest of our hotel, she was entitled to the best care we could possibly provide. I did not leave her side all day and helped with the necessary arrangements of buying medication and calling her family, etc.

The lady eventually returned to the hotel in good health and was welcomed with a beautiful bouquet of flowers. The look in her eyes expressed so much joy and gratitude that I understood that this is the very essence of our work. As an elderly lady, alone in a foreign country and unable to speak the language, this could have been a traumatic situation. However, with a little compassion and sensitivity, the lady knew she had someone she could trust and felt secure in a strange country.

The story, which was written by Rachel Yerushalmi, who works at the hotel, touches upon an important issue. There is no way to prepare employees for every possible problem they will encounter, just as it is impossible to create a process to cover every exception. Despite the false notion that managers are in control, they are actually at the mercy of the Daily Choices their employees make at the moment of truth in front of the customer.

The supporting environment is another important dimension of the story. If the employee did not know that making such decisions is supported by her organization, she would have never made them. Decisions for excellence and going above and beyond will not take roots in an environment that opposes them. Only a well-nurtured environment will cultivate such superior performance. Excellence is a result of a consistently nurtured culture.

This story illustrates that the right environment, one that enables excellence, will lead to exceptional performance. The attention to detail came from simply thinking like the recipient. If you were sick and stuck in a foreign country, what would you want? This is the thinking that Rachel and her staff adopted to avoid delivering a hotel experience and, instead, offer a personal caring experience. They simply treated the guest as they would have loved to be treated. The smile on the guest's face was the ultimate acceptance of their performance. That smile told them they achieved excellence. They followed no rules but their own. They delivered the same excellence they wish someone would deliver to them in sickness—or in health. For them, excellence was not just business, it was personal.

CHAPTER 11

Excellence Daily Choice— Creative Ways to Delight

The Extra That Makes the Difference

Winning contracts is the pursuit of every company. In the business-to-business market, the stakes are higher, but so are the rewards. To win such contracts, companies need to demonstrate a perfect fit with their customers. Deluxe Financial Services has managed to do so with flair and transform the sales process into an extraordinary experience that customers cannot resist.

Deluxe Financial Services prides itself on unparalleled products and solutions, extensive knowledge of consumer preferences, and the ability to transform customer experiences from ordinary to extraordinary. The company, which is known for check-printing services, transformed itself in the last few years into a provider of solutions for the banking industry. As a strategic partner, Deluxe works with banks and credit unions to identify ways to improve operational efficiency, grow revenue, and build stronger, more meaningful relationships with customers.

As Deluxe forges a new path for financial institutions and helps them achieve their most important business goals, the aim to improve satisfaction can seem intangible. Yet, for a mid-size financial institution undergoing a major change—including a new logo and brand image—Deluxe became an unexpected yet ideal partner, demonstrating the value of experience by implementing the practices it endorses.

When a mid-size financial institution initiated a request for suppliers, an unexpected phone call placed Deluxe in the midst of an acquisition bid. Although, initially, Deluxe predicted a less than a 15 percent chance of winning the contract, it developed an innovative and purposefully packaged request for proposal (RFP). Deluxe worked with the financial institution to understand its business philosophy, vision for the future, and most vital business objectives, crafting a truly unique experience for bank executives. The result was a five-year partnership agreement.

From the moment Deluxe began developing the proposal, it focused on fulfilling the needs of the financial institution, capturing its vision, strengthening its new brand image, and building meaningful relationships with its executives and committee members. On several occasions, Deluxe met with key stakeholders to ensure a solid understanding of overall goals and to gain perspective.

In keeping with Deluxe's reputation for helping financial institutions improve customer experiences, each detail of the RFP and presentation process included customized bank details and creative additions to craft a unique experience for the stakeholders:

- Along with the RFP, committee members received a custom "goody" basket containing their favorite snacks and beverages.

- As part of the financial institution's new brand campaign, "in-step and in-tune" with customers, Deluxe delivered handwritten notes to each committee member on musical letterhead. The envelopes were filled with confetti in the shape of music notes.

- The presentation room was preset with the favorite snacks and beverages of each committee member.

- The RFP was hand-delivered rather than shipped through local mail.

- The presentation integrated quotes and ideas from the financial institution's senior leadership team, demonstrating that Deluxe listened to the company's needs.

As part of the new business proposal and presentation, Deluxe organized a visit to the Phoenix Customer Care Center, allowing the financial institution to witness firsthand Deluxe's consistent commitment to the highest quality customer service experience. Deluxe distributed personal invitations to executives and committee members, sending an email reminder the day before departure. While in Phoenix, participants enjoyed first-class accommodations and received welcome gifts in their hotel rooms. Throughout the Customer Care Center tour, Deluxe added customized, personal details to demonstrate the value of a creative and meaningful experience:

- A welcome sign with Deluxe employee signatures greeted the attendees.

- The name of the financial institution and individual committee members flashed and scrolled across overhead message boards, dry erase boards, and computer screens.

- Deluxe employees wore clothes in varying shades of the institution's new logo color—a nontraditional, bold shade of purple. Employees wore purple shirts and purple scarves. One employee even painted his face purple to welcome attendees.

- During lunch, committee members received a CD featuring songs by their favorite artists.

- The financial institution's new logo was carved into the centerpiece at dinner, and its new slogan was written in chocolate around the rim of the dessert plates.

- During the side-by-side live check order placement session with Deluxe associates, committee members were paired with associates having similar interests based on information provided in their bios.

- After the tour, the committee members received a thank-you package that included the welcome sign, photos taken during the tour, and a thank-you letter signed by the associates.

- Throughout the proposal process, Deluxe worked to build meaningful relationships with financial institution executives and create an unforgettable and personalized experience. They demonstrated Deluxe's ability to deepen customer relationships and strengthen brand reputation.

Thinking about the small details such as your customer's preferred colors or songs? Making use of what customers actually say and incorporating it into your sales proposal? Asking your employees to wear the customer's colors? These are small details that go a long way to transform a regular sales process into an experience. It takes intention and *attention* to make it happen. It takes the understanding that every customer is as different as her favorite colors and songs. With a five-year partnership now under way, Deluxe has been able to prove the value of personal service and demonstrate that Deluxe doesn't just talk about outstanding experiences, it delivers. What are your customer's favorite songs?

Delighting Customers One Clip at a Time

And the award for the best (although simplest) way to delight customers goes the Seattle Crowne Plaza Hotel. During my travels, I get to stay in wide variety of hotels around the world. I am often impressed by the many inventions dreamed up by hotels that are geared to enhance the guest experience and add value by solving issues that matter. But the Crowne Plaza Hotel in Seattle impressed me because it managed to solve a problem that even a seasoned guest such as myself did not notice and recognize as a problem. This is a proactive approach that does not wait for customer complaints to dictate the hotel's actions. Instead, the hotel took a proactive approach to anticipate the issues. Kudos!

So you are probably asking, "What is the big invention that impressed me so much?" (I must admit, it is pretty difficult to impress me.) It was a Drape Clip. "What is a Drape Clip?" you ask. I asked the same thing when I first saw a sizable plastic clip called the "Drape Clip" attached to the curtains in the room. After the turndown service, the mystery was solved. The maid used the clip to attach the right and left drapes to ensure complete darkness and prevent even a single ray of sun from entering my room uninvited. At that moment, I realized that most hotel drapes do not close all the way and leave a narrow, yet annoying space between them. This narrow space allows the morning sun's rays to enter and causes guests to wake up earlier than they intended. Once you are awake, it is often difficult to go back to sleep, and you end up feeling tired all day. Someone at the hotel actually thought about the guests and their need for sleep, and tried to place himself in the guest's shoes (or bed), both physically and mentally. Only by doing so could someone have invented the Drape Clip.

Companies often complain that delighting customers and delivering excellence is expensive and eats into their profit margins. They add that their industry is heavily commoditized, and there are no new ideas left to introduce. Both claims may be equally applicable in the hospitality industry; after all, the competition is tough. Many brands compete for guest attention and wallets. The high end of the market includes some fancy perks at a high price that few customers can actually afford. Is great experience a matter of high cost only? No, it does not have to be that way. Great experiences can and should be affordable to reach a greater target audience. The Drape Clip is not too costly. It is not some revolutionary idea that transformed an industry. It is simple. What makes it special is that it reflects the process of thinking like a customer and caring enough to solve the smallest problem.

Unlike popular perception, excellence does not have to be expensive. A simple but creative idea can make all the difference. A company's failure to delight customers has little to do with budget and is often a result of the inability to think like its customers, focusing on the impact to the recipient and not only what the company gains from it. It is more a state of mind than budget size. If you want to start the process of identifying opportunities to delight customers and deliver excellence, try this simple yet imaginative exercise that addresses the following questions:

- "What is the real problem you solve for the customer?" (In the hotel business, it is not just room availability, but rather, executive effectiveness and the importance of sleeping well.)

- "How does the customer consume your products or service?" (Different customers consume products differently.

Search for the bizarre, and you may find some interesting insights.)

- "What else is missing to perfect the total experience?" (Never assume it is complete. The day you declare success is the day you start losing the battle to emerging competitors.)

- "How can I surprise the customer?" (Surprise is what brings the "wow" factor. Meeting expectations is just OK. Do not expect special excitement. Customers will get excited and be willing to pay and remain loyal if you demonstrate the ability to be one step ahead of them, and solve their problems before they even think of them.)

The future belongs to the Drape Clip, a simple yet brilliant application of a cost-effective solution to delight customers. This hotel delivered excellence for less than $1 per room. This is an era where every company struggles to keep costs down and yet find ways to innovate. This could seemingly be a serious conflict. In this case, something that is creatively implemented, something that is simple and brilliant wins over something that is lavish and expensive. Delighting customers and creating memorable, clear differentiation comes from ideas such as the Drape Clip. These ideas demonstrate thinking like the customer and anticipating his needs.

Surprising customers through anticipation is the highest level of excellence. It is solving problems before customers even know and become bothered by them.

Although customers have become more powerful these days, you still have a choice. The choice is either to continue believing the perception that "excellence is expensive" and, as a result, choose the path of no innovation, or to stop acting powerless and take charge of your destiny. Selecting the path of innovation will require different thinking, but it will lead you toward growth and healthier, more profitable customer relationships. Innovation is ultimately about creating excellence and eliminating complacency and parity with competitors. It is a way to differentiate by adding value to customers.

Only you can make the choice to innovate and continue courting customers through new ideas. The future belongs to those companies who can come up with simple, yet brilliant ideas such as Drape Clips that anticipate customer needs and address them. So to get started, let's do a simple exercise. Ask yourself, "What can I do with a regular plastic clip to delight my customers?" Be creative. The power is in the idea. Good luck.

The Old Is Dead—Long Live the Change

I decided to publish the following story as is. I received it from a friend of mine, Kenny Moore, the co-author of *The CEO and the Monk: One Company's Journey to Profit and Purpose* (John Wiley and Sons, 2004). As corporate ombudsman and human resources director at a New York City Fortune 500 energy company, he reports to the CEO and is primarily responsible for awakening joy, meaning, and commitment in the workplace. While these efforts have largely been met with skepticism, he remains eternally optimistic of their future viability.

The story is a great example of creative initiative in time of need or simply making a Daily Choice for excellence. The challenge of change management is daunting, and many companies fail to address it effectively and, therefore, fail to maximize the impact on the change they often must drive. Here is a story about an individual who decided to do it differently and get different results.

Corporate Funerals and the Joy of Change

With all the changes going on in Corporate America, maybe what we all need is a good cry. And what better place to do it than a company funeral? At least, that's the way I tend to look at things. Here's how it all started.

Executives Don't Get It

Awhile back I was working with our corporate executives as my utility company was preparing to stop functioning as a monopoly and begin entering into the throes of deregulation. To jumpstart the process, our CEO implemented an executive goal-setting program and offered employees an early retirement option. Simultaneously, there was also a voluntary severance package given to select areas of the operations. For the first time, we were having a large group of employees exit the company. I was hosting a meeting with the execs to finalize their goals, and they were bemoaning the number of individual retirement parties they were being invited to attend. Eventually, they came to the conclusion that what was needed was one "corporate retirement party" that they all could attend and be done with it. They looked at me and said, "Kenny, please take care of organizing the details." Being low man on the totem pole, I had no choice.

As they continued on in discussion, I mentioned to them that the employees they really needed to have a party with were not the ones that were leaving. "If you're going to celebrate with anyone, it should be with those employees [who] remain behind. It's a better business choice." They looked at me as if I had two heads. "A very interesting thought ... but why don't you leave well enough alone and go get that retirement party set up?" I exited the meeting, went back to my office, and spent the rest of the day cursing their obduracy. So, what else is new?

Change Is Like Marriage ... Only Worse

As the day wore on, I became more compassionate. Maybe they didn't understand what I was talking about and needed a little help in seeing the value of my offer. So I decided to host my own party and invite them for a "look-see." My idea was to design a "Bon Voyage" party ... for the employees who were staying. The underlying thought was that if you worked for me, here's what I'd do to help us face deregulation. I designed the event around the idea that change starts not with a "beginning" but with an "ending." And in-between, there's a "transition" period, where the old rules are gone and the new ones have yet to be defined. While somewhat ambiguous, this period is necessary before any progress is made. We're required to first mourn the loss of the known and spend time wandering around feeling lost and alone. Only then are we ready for a true "beginning."

In corporations, this is somewhat akin to getting married. We may have thought that tying the marital bow was a beginning. But in reality, it ushered in an ending. Life as we knew it was over. We probably weren't aware of it, but our friends were. That's what bachelor parties are all about. The exchanging of vows was a true ending, it just took us a while to catch on. Then, there's the transition. Where do we want to spend the holidays? Kids? How many? If we don't crash, we'll move into the beginning stage of a marriage. Actually, half the marriages never do survive. Somewhat akin to corporate change efforts. Come to think of it, marriage has a higher success rate than most change programs I've seen.

Let the Funeral Begin

For the Bon Voyage party, my plan was to use a large room and invite 40 employees as well as the executive team. I went to the CEO's secretary, told her what I was trying to do and asked if she could get me two hours of his time. She not only got me on his calendar but also notified the other executive secretaries to do the same for their officers. I then sent invitations to a handful of management and union folks, as well as the unsuspecting execs, and made final preparations.

The big day arrived. When people walked in, I had chairs set up in the middle of the room. In three separate corners, I had constructed a scene to depict the stages of change employees would need to travel through: ending, transition, and beginning. Once everyone had arrived, I invited them to take a seat … and we began. "Welcome to our Bon Voyage Party. Many changes are in store for us as we move into deregulation, and this is a chance to visit and celebrate them. I'll ask you to pick up your chairs and come with me to the first leg of our journey … to the section of the room called 'ending.'" Somewhat confused, everyone brought their chairs to the far corner of the room. In this section, I had two large tombstones hung on the wall, remnants from the company's Halloween window display. From the local florist, I ordered a large floral arrangement with a ribbon that read "In loving memory." On a table, I had a small funeral urn and some blank index cards. Before turning on the tape of Gregorian chant, I donned my priestly stole and was ready to begin. (Having spent 15 years in a monastery as a Catholic priest, I wasn't surprised how natural this was all feeling for me.)

"Dearly Beloved: We are gathered here to bid a fond farewell to our company's past. It has served us well ... but alas, we must say goodbye. With proper reverence, let us lay to rest a work life that is over." Most of the group looked puzzled. The CFO turned and asked his fellow exec if he was at the right meeting. I continued: "What I'd like to do is write down on these index cards those things that have ended as we move forward into deregulation." More blank stares. "So, group, what's over for us?" After what seemed like an eternity, one of our union folks spoke up: "You mean, like the lose of job security?"

"Exactly," I said, and wrote it on the index card and dropped it in the funeral urn.

"What else?" Slowly, they got into the swing of things, telling me other things that they felt were over: a stable business environment; the guarantee of secure growth; an end to functioning as a monopoly. One gentleman even said that the future career of the white male was likewise a thing of the past. I wrote it all down and placed it in the urn without comment. Then, I took some "holy" water and blessed it. I explained that while our past needed to be interred with respect, deregulation was inviting us to move forward into the unknown.

Before I led the group to the second corner, I brought out some steamer trunks and added: "Before we leave this burial place, it's important to remember that not everything is over. There are some things that we need to take with us. Let's identify what some of these are. What do we need to bring along from our past that will contribute to our future corporate success?" By now they almost looked like they knew what I was talking about. Some executives were even able to contribute. "A sense of professionalism," said one woman. Another yelled out "teamwork." We were on a roll. In the next few minutes, I filled a handful of cards, threw them in the trunks, and we were ready to move on.

The High Seas of Transition

The next corner represented the transition phase, an ambiguous as well as creative time. In this corner I had hoisted onto the wall a large picture of the Santa Maria from our Columbus Day display—representing that feeling of being disconnected, out there between ports, in this journey called change. As we sat before the boat, I reminded them that we could expect to feel very much like explorers on the high seas: anxious, scared, and uncertain. And just like the first night out on a cruise ship, one of the first things you need to do is don your life vest, go out on deck, and practice for the journey. I then pulled out an uninflated life vest, grabbed someone from the front row, put the deflated vest on him, and asked the group: "What might we as a company do to take care of ourselves during this part of the journey? What would keep us afloat amidst the uncertainty of change?" Like before, they yelled out their answers, I wrote them on index cards, and now stuck them on the life vest to "inflate" it. The group was on to the design. "A sense of humor might help," called out one employee. "Better use of technology," offered another. As the yelling went on, the cards were stuck on the vest, and we were in full swing.

I did another brief exercise about the value of freedom and employee choice during any change effort. It was a take-off from the TV series *Let's Make a Deal* with the group bartering back and forth for what they wanted. It's important to acknowledge that employees can't be forced to change. They can only be invited. This is a different skill set for leaders to learn and it has little semblance to Accounting 101. We spent a few minutes practicing it with the group.

On to the Beginning

Now that we were through with the transition phase, I invited the group to pick up their chairs and move to the final corner of the room: "beginning." This is where the change process culminates. Here, I had a large replica of a stork and baby from our Valentine's Day display. I also had a large sheet cake made up, inscribed: "Congratulations on your new Birth." Chilling in the cooler were bottles of non-alcoholic champagne for the toast, which I would use to end the program. (My company has a "no alcohol" policy that forced me to serve cider. When I was in the monastery, at least I was able to drink! Another grim reminder that corporate life can be more restrictive than the monastic one.)

In the beginning phase of change, companies focus on the future. I broke the crowd into smaller groups and gave each a large sheet of paper with crayons. I instructed them to draw a picture of what they wanted our company's future to look like. "Use images and symbols to represent your thoughts." Walking around the room, I saw primitive artists capturing their group's thoughts. After 10 minutes, they held up their drawings and explained what their images all meant. I made no comment, but went to passing out the cake and champagne. "I raise a toast to this new vision that you've created. Similar to the birth of a child, the future still remains uncertain, and there's no surety of long life. But the sharing of food and drink represents the community's belief and support for that future. Working together, our hope is that it will flourish."

Examining the Process

With the formal toast, the event was over. I explained that if they worked for me, this is how I'd go about involving them with deregulation. While it need not be a party, it was nonetheless important to find a way of celebrating and recognizing the changes before us. "What did you think of this event and the journey I took you on?" One woman commented that she felt more hopeful in hearing other employees speak positively about the company's future. Another shared his feelings of loss that the company he had spent his whole career in was going to change forever. At one point, the CEO spoke up: "This is the kind of thing we need to do more of. It's very much in line with where I'm trying to take us. Kenny, I'd like you to present this at next month's executive session for all our managers to see. ..." With minor changes, I took the show on the road and moved it to our auditorium for a crowd of 300. The discussion there was even livelier. As we moved the company into deregulation, this event served as a corporate symbol. Life for us had changed. While we had gained some things, we had lost others. And we were able to become more accommodating to employees' sense of grief as well as their excitement for change.

Postmortem

We're now well into deregulation and have merged with other companies to grow our business. Throughout this journey, we've learned that change starts with an ending.

And we're well served by bringing affected employees together to talk about what's been lost, and acknowledge and treat it with respect before moving on. We're also becoming aware that moving employees from compliance to commitment is not just about offering more money. It's about an entirely different conversation. One that feels more like an invitation than a command. And we have much work still to do here. Likewise, we're no longer blind to the great creativity that's present in the transition phase of any change. The priest in me is still occasionally called out of retirement to host another funeral in the life of the corporate community. The cycle of life, death, and rebirth seems to never end.

I'm thinking that my next plan might be to find a way for the Sacrament of Confession to become part of the performance appraisal program. Who knows, maybe saying "Bless me, boss—for I have sinned ..." and identifying my own contribution to the problems I gripe about is a good way to start the annual review process? Perhaps the Divine might even look down and bestow Her warm forgiveness upon me? But something tells me I still wouldn't get the big raise I deserve.

I'm sure some business folks will refrain from hosting a ceremony, falsely believing that you can't do this kind of work if you're not a priest. Wrong! Rituals and ceremonies are part of the human experience and predate organized religion by thousands of years. Besides, you don't need to have lived in a monastery to craft a ritual to meet pressing business needs. The pain and imperfections in the corporate world are an ever-present invitation for us to take some risks, improvise a human ceremony that supports the work at hand, and encourage employees to respond with wit and valor.

Others might balk at the impossibility of effectively nurturing the human spirit in bureaucratic corporations. And for these people, I have a compassionate understanding of this challenge. However, one of the things I learned in the monastery was that just because something is impossible, doesn't mean you don't have to work on it. (Why else would I have been required to take the vow of celibacy?) Some of what we are required to work on will not be accomplished in our lifetimes. That's what vision, brilliance, and legacy is about. To those needing encouragement, I give you the words of my old religious superior: If you think you're too small to be effective, then you've never been in bed with a mosquito. We all can have an impact, even if it's a small one.

The poet Theodore Roethke said it well: "What we need is more people who specialize in the impossible." The challenges are formidable, yet the need is great. Life invites us daily to take the risk and act on making the impossible happen. It's at the heart of what makes showing up for work so exciting.

Kenny took the initiative as an individual who wanted to do it differently to achieve different results. He unleashed the power of creativity and surprise to create excellence. Kenny focused on the people and their feelings to design an effective program that will mobilize change and make people embrace it. By recognizing the issues and fears of the recipients, he designed a creative and effective method to deal with change management. He transformed the traditional top-down meeting into a meaningful exercise where the recipients were recognized, respected, and placed at the heart of the matter.

This story and practice can come out of respect for and recognition of people's emotions. Change can bring many negative fears, but it can also ignite new hopes. Without recognizing those fears and addressing them, the hopes and excitement will not take place. Kenny recognized that change is not a matter of reviewing the agenda and making sure everyone is on board. It is about dissemination and addressing head on the open issues and fears associated with the change. There is no special approval required—just think about the faces of the people in your office when they see you conducting a funeral for the old ways of doing business. The message will be loud and clear.

Creating Customer Compliments in Five Minutes

What can you achieve in five minutes? Most would say not much. Well, Ronen Nissenbaum creates excellence, five minutes at a time.

Running a 422-room luxury hotel with 400 employees is no small task. As the general manager of the InterContinental Hotel in Atlanta, Georgia, Ronen's agenda is extremely busy. And yet he finds time to develop special practices that will make a difference every day. Unlike many hotels, where the human resources manager and the direct supervisor interview prospective employees, Ronen instituted a special requirement in his hotel in which *every* new recruit in his hotel would be spending five minutes with him before being hired.

Although five minutes might not seem like a long time, it is long enough to let Ronen deliver a personal message to his new employees. Success is not measured by attempts; success will not be measured by fulfilling customer's requests. In Ronen's world, there is only one measure of success: customer compliments. He also clearly understands that to achieve compliments, you need to go above and beyond basic skills. Skills create parity but not excellence; excellence is in the eye of the beholder. You need the recipient to define your excellence. We can obtain compliments only when we raise the bar of our standards to meet the bar set by our customers. For Ronen, the customer bar was set very high; serving the most discerning and demanding customers comes with high expectations. Success must pass the ultimate test at Atlanta's InterContinental Hotel: impressing some of the most discerning guests. It is only when guests are impressed that they will compliment, and the guests do not dispense compliments easily. It takes a pretty phenomenal performance to impress them.

Understanding this fundamental difference, Ronen does not just send a memo to the employees, he personally delivers the message to each and every one. This personal meeting with each employee is a major burden on his already crowded schedule, but for him, it is a well-made investment.

"You wouldn't believe the enthusiasm this generates: Can you imagine, where most places the employees don't even get to see the general manager, let alone talk to them or get interviewed by them. Employees feel extremely special, and we get much better results that ripple through the organization," said Ronen.

By taking the time to meet with each employee, Ronen is also sending a strong message about the importance of each employee's performance. By not missing any employee, Ronen is highlighting how much the hotel depends on personal commitment to excellence.

It only takes five minutes, but in that time, Ronen manages to create excellence in his organization. He raises the bar of excellence by defining it in the context of customer compliments. It is not an instant formula. It is a discipline that recognizes that you are as good as the weakest link in your organization. It is an admission and acceptance of the fact that you are only as good as what the recipients are willing to say about you, not your subjective and often too supportive view of your performance. Every employee's Daily Choice can tip the scale from excellence to mediocrity. In the business of compliments, mediocrity is not an option. Neither is consistent yet boring service. In the business of compliments, it is excellence or nothing, and every compliment counts. That is why Ronen makes sure he keeps his five-minute appointments.

The five-minute rule, combined with setting standards for customer compliments, is a practice every manager can easily adopt. The resistance may stem from the fear of not getting too many compliments, which often implies that your "good" is not good enough. If you do not have five minutes for each employee, then you jeopardize the competitiveness of your organization. If you are too afraid to subject yourself and your excellence definition to customer compliments, you are actually sending your customers straight to your competitors. Ronen made the choice. The moment those compliments start coming, you will see that they are all worth the effort. There is nothing more thrilling than authentic gratitude from a customer.

CHAPTER **12**

Excellence
Daily Choice—
Wow!

All You Need Is Love ... in 11 Languages

If you think love is difficult, try expressing it in 11 different languages at once. "Attitude is the hardest thing to get," according to Jane Onderwater from HECC in the village of Boxtel in The Netherlands. HECC is a pan-European contact center, which services customers in 11 different languages. But love is actually a central focus of the people at HECC.

Jane and her colleagues know that answering a call is not difficult. Communicating love, however, is what makes all the difference. Living with love became central to everything they do. So, despite the fact that Valentine's Day is not celebrated in Holland, they decided to celebrate it at HECC. On Valentine's Day, the company gives gifts to spouses of the employees. This form of appreciation recognizes that the spouse is supporting the employee as part of a much bigger family.

Such acts of love go a long way. Many times, employees bring their spouses to work at HECC. "We live from love," Jane added. Often

173

Dutch employees who travel the world will fall in love with a foreigner and bring them to Holland. Once there, they become a perfect match for HECC employee profiles because they bring foreign languages and understanding of other cultures into the center—understanding that is critical to HECC's success.

Some people may associate love with a casual environment and lack of accountability in one of those "free for all" cultures. But make no mistake, HECC is here to make money. Love is simply their secret weapon to get it done. In fact, accountability and involvement reach new heights in HECC's loving environment. Being well-attuned to the business objectives of the company, HECC ensures every employee is accountable. HECC involves every employee in the selling process. Every employee, including the people working at the cafeteria, will be engaged in responding to sales queries and creating sales proposals. By having every employee be a part of the creation of a sales proposal, they get exposed to the challenges of winning a customer. The difficulties in winning the deal reinforce how important delivering great experiences and performing are at the excellence level. At that level, love becomes a supporter of excellence and not permission for loose performance.

If your employees experience the challenge and difficulties of the selling process, their commitment to excellence will change dramatically. Employee focus on the customers will be sharpened. It is only after you experience the difficulty in winning a customer that you will work twice as hard to keep him.

Why is love so important? It's not just because it symbolizes caring; love, in HECC terminology, is adding value to benefit the customer. It goes beyond sympathy and into tangible benefits that each employee offers to customers.

Love is a great concept that usually generates fear in corporations. Many executives squirm when the word "love" is mentioned. But love is the most authentic way to connect and delight customers. In some ways, you actually already count on employees' love (by expecting them to be caring, creative, sincere, and customer-centric); you just didn't refer to it by this name. Love helps us rise above consistency and deliver excellence. Love helps your employees care about the impact their performance makes on the recipient of their work. When we love what we do and love where we do it, we do our best. HECC realized that if you want to be successful and competitive, you need to start by spreading the love and not taking customers for granted.

Excelling at the Smallest Details

When speaking to Alaric DaCunha, the manager of the Fairmont President Club at the Fairmont Royal York hotel in Toronto, you get the sense that there is much more to his job than what his title may imply. The best description would probably be Chief Spoiling Officer. Alaric is responsible for delighting the hotel's most demanding customers. He gets them what they want when they want it and often without their even asking for it.

Working with demanding customers is difficult. Satisfying their needs is not easy either. But that is just not enough. Surprising customers by exceeding expectations is what Alaric does for a living every day. He achieves this excellence performance level by mastering one of the oldest yet most proven skills of them all: listening.

The Fairmount President Club program allows every guest to register their specific preferences including pillow type, preferred room, and preferred distance from the elevator. This practice is common in many hotels that attempt to please loyal customers. But the Fairmont hotel chain has gone a step further. The hotels keep detailed records of *every* request or comment that a guest has ever made and holds a record of it for the guest's next arrival. Let's say that during a meal at the restaurant, a guest mentions that she is lactose intolerant. The waiter will not only address the request but will also submit the request so it can be recorded in the guest profile. The next time the guest checks in at any of the Fairmont hotels, the staff will be ready for that request. Using a simple "preference note pad," Fairmont employees record every special customer request and submit them to be included in the guest's profile. A simple pad of paper and the intention to make every stay comfortable and personal are at the core of the special service the hotel chain delivers.

When Alaric arrives at work, he receives a list of all the guests scheduled to arrive in the next three days and their special preferences that were collected and recorded by Fairmont employees around the world. He reviews the special requests with each department, making sure the staff is ready to deliver the personal whims of every guest. Require a humidifier in your room? You can count on it. Need six bottles of water at night (yes, it is a real request)? They will be there. One hotel guest insists on having four feather pillows, an extra robe, and extra toilet paper and tissues. Alaric does not ask questions. He simply makes sure it will be there. When a guest prefers to have a 7 AM breakfast reservation every morning, Alaric makes sure it will happen before the guest even asks. Guests just need to ask for it once, and Alaric will make sure it will be remembered for all future stays in any of the Fairmont hotels.

Anticipating expectations, listening to needs, and delivering products and services before being asked are important parts of Alaric's job. Customers recognize it and refer to his hotel as home. This is the highest compliment Alaric can get.

But mistakes can happen. Guests may encounter a problem that will displease them. For Alaric, those problems are opportunities. He will relentlessly contact the customer and make sure the matter is resolved. Dealing with busy customers, Alaric sometimes has to try six to seven times before he reaches them. But hassles do not deter Alaric. A simple email may do the trick, but he knows that the personal contact to speak about the problem is valuable, and he sees how the guests usually return as a result of this approach.

"The greatest reward is listening to a guest thanking us for the service we give them," Alaric says. He once received an email from a customer stating, "The stay will spoil me for all future stays!!!"

Listening to customers, keeping track of the smallest preference details, and anticipating customer needs in advance are at the core of how Alaric and the Fairmont hotels make a difference and deliver excellence. They do not deliver standardized excellence (there is really no such thing); they deliver *differentiating* excellence. They recognize that excellence is defined differently by different customers. For some, excellence is an extra tissue box; for others, it is a prearranged reservation for breakfast. However a guest defines excellence, Alaric is there to ensure that it is delivered by any employee of the hotel.

Alaric provides one suggestion to others: "Use their name." Customers like to be called by their names. It is a simple gesture that goes a long way and demonstrates that you care for them as unique individuals. When people check in, it is common for the doorman to peek at the luggage tag and radio the guests' names to the reception desk, so that when the guests approach the desks to check in, they will be welcomed personally by name. Just imagine the surprise on their face as they declare, "How did you know my name?"

How far would Alaric go to deliver excellence in the smallest details? One guest apparently dislikes waiting five minutes for the valet parking attendant. As a result, each time the guest is expected to arrive, Alaric arranges for someone to wait for this guest and pick up his car immediately, a small gesture that means excellence to this specific guest.

The Sweet Taste of Everything

Chocolate on your pillow has become an extinct benefit of staying at hotels. Most hotels stopped providing this small, tasty perk as part of cost-reduction efforts. But the Renaissances Hotel in Mumbai, India, took a different approach. The hotel showers its guests with miniature versions of Mars and Snickers bars at every opportunity: chocolate with your messages, chocolate with your dry cleaning, chocolate at the concierge, chocolate on the pillow, and chocolate after cleaning the room.

Everywhere guests go or interact with the hotel, a small chocolate will be waiting for them. Talk about sweetening the deal! Hotel guests end up with a sizable collection of chocolates by the end of their stay. From a cost standpoint, I doubt these chocolates are too expensive, but their impact far exceeds the cost. The abundance in which they are distributed indicates generosity that simply brings the "wow" factor and puts a smile on the face of each guest.

The chocolate represents the human touch, connection, and generosity, a symbol of going beyond the call of duty. What in your customer experience demonstrates generosity? What symbolizes the attitude of going beyond the call of duty? How do you show caring at the basic human level? With a simple creative gesture, the Renaissance in Mumbai connects to customers with a touch they all can relate to and appreciate.

Chocolate does not have to be expensive, and yet it sends a small yet powerful message of generosity and caring. The smell and taste of the sweets engage guests and create smiles. And those smiles are what excellence is all about for the guests of the Renaissance Mumbai. They pack excellence in small chocolate packages.

A Courier for a Day or Redefining On-Time

There are many objective, out-of-control reasons why certain things do not happen the way they should. We may have no control over weather delays, acts of God, or missing a deadline. But those reasons should not stop us from finding creative ways to circumvent the out-of-control circumstances and still delight customers. This is exactly what Raffaela Fehr did.

Mr. X, a customer in Switzerland, was expecting an urgently needed partnership agreement from a company in New York. Due to the urgent nature of the document, it was sent via FedEx on Thursday, March 24 for next-day delivery in Switzerland. But because of bad weather at the Newark International Airport on March 24, FedEx faced a severe delay that was beyond its control, and this resulted in a delay of the outbound flight from the U.S. to Paris. This delay caused Mr. X's agreement to be stuck in Newark. Since Friday, March 25, and the following Monday were part of the Easter holidays in Switzerland, Mr. X's shipment didn't go out for delivery until the next Tuesday. The shipment was addressed to his home, but because he was at work on Tuesday, the courier had to leave an "attempted delivery" slip at Mr. X's house.

On March 30, Mr. X's assistant called, asking if FedEx could reroute this urgently needed partnership agreement to his business address, since he was leaving on a business trip at 9 the next morning. Or could FedEx redeliver it before 8:45 the next morning to his home? Unfortunately, the call was made too late to redeliver on March 30, and while an early delivery the next morning was feasible, it would require Mr. X to pay for special delivery.

Up until this point, it was not FedEx's fault that the partnership agreement package had not reached Mr. X. A series of unfortunate events ranging from bad weather to not being at home to calling after the delivery cut-off time were all to blame. But good reasons did not deliver the package on time to Mr. X.

Raffaela Fehr, a FedEx customer care agent in Zurich, was assigned to the trace and took control of this urgent delivery. She realized that if she were in Mr. X's position, she would be willing to pay for a special delivery early the next morning, but she would prefer to avoid these extra costs. In fact, she would prefer to have the agreement in hand that evening before leaving. Raffaela was thinking like the customer. She placed herself in Mr. X's shoes and tried to imagine his predicament, as well as his wish for complete resolution.

Since Raffaela had an appointment later that evening near Mr. X's home, she decided to pick up the shipment at the station and deliver it herself. By doing so, she would save Mr. X the extra fee and deliver the package earlier. This was exactly how she would have liked the situation to be resolved if this happened to her. She asked her manager for permission to execute this "special, personal delivery," went over to the station to get the shipment, and informed Mr. X that he would receive his shipment about 9 PM. She drove to his village in her private car, showed her FedEx badge, and finally delivered the shipment to Mr. X's wife at 8:45 on the evening before Mr. X left Switzerland.

Mr. X was absolutely delighted that a FedEx employee, other than a courier, took charge of his package and delivered it personally to his home address in the evening, outside of her usual working hours.

It did not matter that Raffaela was not officially a courier of FedEx. It did not matter that it was not her fault or responsibility. It did not matter that she used her own car. It did not matter that it was outside of her normal hours. To Raffaela, only one thing mattered: She took the initiative because she focused on the ultimate impact on the customer. She rose to a higher standard and treated Mr. X the way she would have loved to be treated, with a touch of caring and excellence.

Who Is Dr. WOW?

No one has ever seen Dr. WOW in person, but people at Commerce Bank know he is real. The Cherry Hill, New Jersey, bank is known for the special approach he uses for customer service. The bank is generous with its customers and treats them with an above-and-beyond attitude. After all, how many banks do you know that love their customers enough to give away 21 million free pens, 9 million free lollipops, and 2 million free dog biscuits every year? To keep this special attitude of excellence and customer care, the bank invented Dr. WOW, a specialist in how to wow customers. Employees approach him with questions regarding problems and ask for his advice. Dr. WOW will reply with suggestions and ideas on how to wow the customers.

But keeping a spirit of excellence is difficult when customers complain. The reality is that employees encounter more upset customers than delighted ones during their work. Such encounters can drag down spirits and erode the commitment to excellence. Here comes Dr. WOW, who keeps the spirit of excellence high by sending employees several announcements every week. When a customer sends a thank-you letter, Dr. WOW will send a quote from it and celebrate the success created by the bank for this customer. If an employee took the initiative to create a great customer experience, you can count on Dr. WOW to spread the message. The goal is to raise the spirits of employees with examples of how to wow customers and ensure that the spirit and the commitment to excellence stay high. Keeping the standards of performance beyond parity and at the excellence level is the top item on Dr. WOW's agenda. Some might find the idea of Dr. WOW corny. But the results speak for themselves. The doctor no one ever sees seems to have a very strong and real presence in making employees believers and customers raving fans.

Who owns excellence in your organization? Who is the chief cheerleader who defends you from inertia and cynicism? How do you inspire your people every day and ensure that success is celebrated and not taken for granted? Dr. WOW is not just an anecdote or a strange whim of some executive. Instead, it is a serious recognition of the threat of cynicism and the importance of high morale. It represents Commerce Bank's commitment to keep excellence constant and keep that high standard. It might sound funky and a bit off the chart, but how do you make sure excellence is delivered every day by everyone?

A Beary Passionate Place to Be

Anyone who visits Build-A-Bear Workshop notices right away that there is something special in the air. It is a place like no other. The spirit and ambience of Build-A-Bear Workshops exude happiness. From the moment you are welcomed in the store to the general attitude of every interaction with employees to the fluffy bears you create, it is a passionate, happy experience. Without realizing it, your face muscles shift and you find yourself smiling. You are happy to be here. To unlock the Build-A-Bear Workshop magic and learn form its unique practices, we asked Maxine Clark, founder and chief executive bear of Build-A-Bear Workshop, to share her recipe for happiness creation, one employee at a time, one customer at a time.

What are the hiring criteria to identify the right person to work at Build-A-Bear Workshop?

We look for a number of things when considering a candidate, such as passion, enthusiasm, dedication, a can-do attitude, and an overall willingness to do any job. Passion is very important in a potential candidate; I have learned that to be happy and successful in business, you must do work you are passionate about.

How does empowerment play at your organization? What type of authority do people have? At what level?

We are a "Yes" company—that is our standard operating procedure manual, so to speak. Empowering employees to make decisions and try new things is very important. It's essential to give workers license to take risks without fear of failure or management's wrath. At Build-A-Bear Workshop, we tend to be right more than we are wrong, but mistakes do happen. We encourage associates to think of every so-called mistake as one step closer to getting things right.

How is excellence recognized and rewarded?

Positive recognition is essential to a happy and productive workforce. If an associate does something super special—and this happens all the time—we'll reward them with lots of fanfare and hoopla. In fact, we've designated September as Bear Builder Appreciation Month. It's our official way of paying tribute to the associates who are the reason for our success all year-round. We give out awards and honor associates with gifts and paid days off. October is We Appreciate Managers Month, and similar celebrations are held for our store management teams. Build-A-Bear Workshop has found employee appreciation months to be an excellent way to show that we value them above and beyond.

Please provide an example of a unique employee initiative.

Creating a fun place for our employees to work is a priority for Build-A-Bear Workshop. Some of the unique employee initiatives we offer include the following:

- Bring your dog to work (any day or every day) at World Bearquarters

- A casual dress code

- An extra day off during the month of your birthday

- Creative titles, such as Chief Executive Bear for our CEO

- Celebration of milestones for the company and our associates

How do employees deal with difficult situations, such as an unsatisfied guest?

At Build-A-Bear Workshop, we follow the golden rule: Treat others as you want to be treated and say "Yes" to guests. Our motto is give honey to others as you would like it given to you. Our associates are empowered to make decisions in the best way to create a highly satisfied guest. If there is an unsatisfied guest, we will immediately remedy the situation and ensure that the guest leaves satisfied. The experience guests have in our stores is what sets us apart from other retailers.

I personally receive thousands of letters from guests who want to share their experiences with me. We take guest feedback to heart and implement their feedback/suggestions in everything we do.

How do you make people love bears and keep the spirit up?

It's the experience! We offer an experience, not just a furry friend. We like to believe that guests who enter Build-A-Bear Workshop stores are really getting their stuffed animals for free and are paying for their experience in our stores. Our highly visual and colorful stores feature a teddy bear theme, displays of numerous, fully dressed stuffed animals, and the selective use of special "bear" phrases such as "A hug is worth a thousand words" and "Be the bearer of good news" decorate the walls of our stores.

Our stores also include custom-designed features with larger-than-life details, including a moving Sentry Bear holding a large needle at the store's doorway, an exaggerated bathtub where our guests can fluff their new stuffed animals, and a 10-foot-tall zipper column in the dressing area. Cheerful proprietary teddy bear music plays in our stores and the sign system is easy to read to distinguish each station and direct the guests through the animal-making process. Guests are met at the store entrance by our "First Impressions Bear" who introduces our concept and our collection of furry stuffed animals. At each station, a friendly and knowledgeable Bear Builder associate is available to explain the process.

Please provide examples of how Build-A-Bear Workshop became involved in a special project—hospital or needy kids to bring out the Build-A-Bear Workshop spirit.

Build-A-Bear Workshop has focused our charitable efforts on those causes that matter most to our guests and their families, especially those causes that benefit children. We have several animals—Nikki's Bear, Bearemy's Kennel Pals friends, and Read Teddy—that are associated with specific causes and charities. Whenever a guest buys one of these lovable creatures, a portion of the proceeds is donated to that cause. We recently introduced our third Nikki's Bear, which is named for 14-year-old Nikki Giampolo. Nikki loved life, children, and teddy bears. She shared that love by giving bears and hugs to all those around her. Sadly, Nikki lost her battle with cancer in 2002. But her courage and spirit live on. Nikki's mom and friends shared her story of hope with us. Her good works inspired us to create Nikki's Bear to help other children with cancer. We've since expanded our giving to include other children's health and wellness causes important to our guests, such as juvenile diabetes and autism.

We also have a series of World Wildlife Fund (WWF) animals, and those sales support efforts to protect endangered animals and their habitats. We've raised more than $1 million for WWF so far! And our Bearemy's Kennel Pals have generated more than $2 million for pet programs across the country and in Canada.

As we can see from Maxine's words, there is no one big secret that is added to the Build-A-Bear Workshop formula. It is rather a series of small actions that adds up to a complete passionate experience. It starts with small steps such as the conscious choice to refer to customers as guests. (We treat guests differently and usually with great respect. We like having guests.) By dedicating time to appreciate employees and managers and focusing all efforts on delighting guests, Build-A-Bear Workshop stores build a place everyone wants to be part of as an employee or as a customer. The secret to the happy experiences of Build-A-Bear Workshop is the everyday behavior, the Daily Choices employees make to delight guests and deliver excellence in everything they do.

CHAPTER 13

Excellence
Daily Choice
in Difficult Times

Redefining "Getting It Done"

Adam Wirt is a loan officer at HomeBanc's office in Charlotte, North Carolina. When it comes to getting the job done, Adam operates by his own set of standards. While some people define their jobs in the context of loans, Adam defines his differently. He is always working diligently to help customers obtain the loans that will help them buy the house of their dreams. But in one case, working diligently took on special meaning for Adam. He was working on a loan for a veteran borrower who needed a quick turnaround. Despite his efforts, the required appraisal for the loan approval arrived too late and indicated that some last-minute repairs were required before the loan could be approved.

The real estate agent's original plan was to hire a handyman to take care of the repairs. Meanwhile, Adam discovered that the customer was living in his car until the loan closed and he could move into his new home. That's when Adam took the matter into his own hands. He simply could not see another human being living out of a car and knew something needed to be done.

"After looking through the list of repairs that were needed, I thought there wasn't anything on there I could not handle myself," Adam said. He went home, collected his sawhorse and tools, stopped at Home Depot to purchase supplies, and then went to work. He worked for seven hours until well after dark to finish the repairs in one day to minimize any delay. Adam repaired a gated fence that had been torn off its hinges, fixed window seals that had dry-rotted, and cleaned the carpet, as the appraiser required. His goal was to allow the customer to close the loan as soon as possible and move out of his car and into his new home. To avoid any last-minute glitches during the closing, Adam took photos documenting the completed repairs, which served as evidence that the house was ready for closing.

"I don't think I did something out of the ordinary—99 percent of our HomeBanc associates would have done the same thing," he claimed. "I've always felt like I had a voice here and I've felt like everyone was willing to help out in any situation, be it professional or personal," Adam said. He attributes his actions to the unique environment in the bank, one fueled by people who genuinely care and make it the most natural behavior in the world.

For Adam, getting the job done was redefined. He focused on the complete needs of the customer. In a narrow definition, Adam got his job done when the loan was prepared. Technically, the repairs were the customer's problem and were not part of Adam's job description. The customer did not even expect it. But Adam defines a job well done only from the strictest criteria of solving the customer's problem. He knew that if the customer was in need, the job was not done. Only when the customer moved into his new house did the job get completed. It is this perspective of ownership, responsibility, and pride to be of service that made fixing the customer's future house free of charge the most natural thing for him to do.

Combining personal caring with a strong commitment to excellence, Adam simply got the repair jobs done. No manager needed to ask him to do it. He simply knew what excellence is all about and redefined "job well done" in the process. Like Adam, can you see the customer needs beyond the defined task? Do you fully understand the bigger picture your customer is facing? It is taking ownership of this big picture and adding a personal touch of caring for a customer in distress that created the excellence Adam delivered.

With Patience and Perseverance

When three packages arrived with only the name Xeicon as the identifying information to Flying Cargo's warehouse in Petach Tikva, Israel, the challenge was quite serious. No recipient or shipper information was provided. Flying Cargo, a FedEx licensee in Israel, had a choice: It could ignore the problem and wait for someone to claim the packages or be proactive. After all, it was irresponsible for the shipper to send three packages without a full address or even the shipper's information. So it was not technically Flying Cargo's fault if the packages never made it to the unknown recipient. But Daniel Kloghaft, a Flying Cargo employee, was not one who waits for others. The unknown shipments did not represent an excuse for him, but rather, it became a personal challenge.

Daniel engaged in a thorough search to find "Xeicon" and figure out what should be done with the packages. He visited all the Web sites that contained the term "Xeicon" and submitted questions to every address he could find, requesting information about the unidentified packages. Most of the responses he received didn't have knowledge about the packages, but Daniel did not give up.

Eventually, Daniel received a positive response. A person by the name of Jeff Webber claimed that the packages belonged to him, but he was not sure which shipment they were part of. With permission, Daniel opened the packages and took photos of the contents with his digital camera and sent them to Jeff for identification. Jeff recognized the packages as part of a larger shipment he sent. He provided Daniel with further information that helped him identify the shipments. By this time, the Israeli customer who was waiting for those shipments called and claimed his missing packages, which turned out to be part of a large shipment that had already been delivered. The three missing boxes included accessories that were supposed to be shipped and delivered with the main package, but somehow got left behind. The shipment finally made it to the intended customer.

The entire search process took two-and-a-half months. Talk about commitment! But Daniel's perseverance won over the day. He took the challenge personally, despite the excuses that it was not his fault or responsibility. Daniel did not let any of the obstacles along the way stop his efforts. Though the delay was not his fault, he remembered that for every package, there is a recipient who is waiting for the package. It was this recipient and his need for the package that motivated him to stick to his efforts on this two-and-a-half-month journey until the problem was resolved. Sometimes excellence takes a long time to complete, but the greater the challenge, the greater the triumph.

Everyone Listens to Customers

There is nothing more powerful than listening to your customers. A simple message delivered in the voice of the customer can be more insightful than hundreds of pie charts and Excel spreadsheets. Listening to customers is a corporate mantra every executive loves to tout, but few executives can actually live by it. Time limitations and general attitude cause many executives to neglect this important responsibility. Executives often cannot find the time between all the internal meetings to speak to customers. Neglecting the responsibility of listening to customers can make companies self-centered and removed from customer needs and wishes.

When executives are asked to join customer discussions at the call center, they are often pressed for time and decline. Executives always seem to have some higher-priority issues to handle than to listen to those who pay the bills. Even when executives finally go meet customers, the visits are staged, and the agenda is predetermined so that the real voice of the customer is never heard.

When "Paul," vice president of customer service at a Fortune 500 corporation, faced the challenge, he came up with a creative solution. He decided that if the executives would not come to the customers, he would bring the customers to the executives. Using readily available technologies, he started to record customer interactions at his call centers and then create CDs with selected calls. The CDs were then distributed to executives, who could listen to them while on the way to work or during down times. Titled "Our Greatest Hits," the CDs were popular and in demand. "It was painful to listen to those calls," one of the executives said, "but it opened my eyes to the way customers think and speak about us."

Following the initial success, Paul made the CDs a regular part of the executive agenda at the corporation. Every two to three weeks, a new "Our Greatest Hits" CD was produced with fresh customer comments. Using this simple idea, Paul brought the executives together to think like customers and ultimately shape their decisions to fit customer needs. The impact the CDs created was quite strong. People got used to incorporating the customers into their daily thinking and decisions by listening to live customers.

This story of excellence is easy to copy. Most call centers today are equipped with recording technologies. Getting every employee exposed to the voice of the customer is a great exercise in shaping the thinking and decision making of the organization, helping the company to be fully tuned to the customer's way of thinking. Going beyond graphs and spreadsheets, employees get to hear real customers who express real feelings and emotions. It is a painful experience to hear an upset customer calling your products "names," but it can also be the best wake-up call. Alternatively, it is thrilling to hear customers describe how they enjoy your product and provide some insight for new, innovative ideas. Listening to these voices allows executives to adapt their language and way of thinking to that of their customers. It is all there in the unprocessed, real voice of the customer, expressed in the most human way.

Paul did not let the obstacles of executives' availability or reluctance stop him. Since he could not bring the executives to the customers, he simply brought the customers to the executives. And sometimes that is what it takes to change an entire organization's perspective and to cultivate a focus on excellence through delighting customers. To deliver excellence that is based on the recipient, you need to know your customer better than they know themselves. The practice of listening to customers must be performed regularly. You need to be well-versed in your customers' lifestyles, challenges, aspirations, and fears to best design and deliver that excellence they are striving for, the excellence that will truly solve their problem. Paul's creativity enabled him to make everyone listen to their customers, and know how to delight them and deliver excellence.

Chainsaw and the Art of Amazing Customer Experiences

Smashing guitars has been a fixture of the music industry for decades. Every musician who thinks he has reached a certain status cements that status by trashing a guitar on stage in some bizarre ritual of acceptance and arrival. But Henry Juskiewicz gave the old tradition a new twist and probably a new meaning.

When Henry acquired Gibson Guitar in 1985, he faced a company with a great heritage near collapse. In a recent interview with *USA Today*, Henry disclosed one of the steps he took to turn around the flagging company. To reinforce the concept of product excellence, Henry took a faulty guitar that was destined to be sold as a "second," and, in the presence of the company's employees, he smashed the guitar and declared that as of that moment, any guitar that did not meet the standard of a first-class Gibson guitar would not be sold to customers. Seconds with some blemishes or subtle problems were common in the industry and were sold as "good enough" guitars. Henry would rather see these guitars destroyed than in the hands of customers. To emphasize his philosophy, he instructed employees to smash each faulty guitar. All smashed guitars were piled in a designated area during the week. At the end of every week, he would lead his employees by using a chainsaw to destroy the faulty guitars and ensure that they would never end up in the hands of customers.

To many, this procedure may sound theatrical and harsh. Finance people would likely argue that by smashing guitars that can be sold as seconds, the company loses out on a potential revenue stream. They would argue that defects in these guitars are rarely noticeable and would not impede a customer's guitar playing. But Henry realized a deeper truth: However tempting it may be to capture additional revenue from the sale of faulty or defective products, one cannot sell seconds and deliver amazing customer experiences. The impact on brand image and on the customer experience will ultimately be devastating.

While destroying guitars with a chainsaw may be a painful sight, this action sends two critical messages. For employees, the message is that Gibson Guitar is a "no-excuses" experience and that anything less than perfection will not be tolerated. When you accept "seconds," it becomes difficult to get first-rate guitars. Any compromise in quality leads to an overall compromise in excellence. Product superiority is a competitive and strategic advantage and selling faulty guitars, however minute those faults may be, erodes that advantage. Furthermore, tolerating seconds will lead employees to accept less than the highest standards. Production standards will ultimately decline, and the customer experience will be diminished. A subsequent reduction in profits and a decline in customer loyalty will soon follow.

The message to customers centered on the company's high product standards. By witnessing product excellence each time customers bought or played a guitar, they would know that Gibson Guitar provides only the very best. Customer expectations would be exceeded, and their experiences would be delightful. By destroying faulty guitars, Henry was destroying any attitude of taking customers for granted. It would make no difference if faulty guitars were offered at a discount or even clearly marked as being faulty—the brand would still be tarnished and Gibson guitars would be seen as less than perfect.

A commitment to excellence is predicated on offering only first-class products and never allowing anything less than first-class products to reach the market. This unwavering commitment to quality ensured that Gibson delivered excellence and ultimately delighted its customers.

A short-term view will often lead executives to increase revenue by selling flawed or second-class products. Many companies succumb to this temptation, and their myriad products can be purchased in outlet malls nationwide. While revenue may actually increase, the effect of selling flawed or second-rate products on the organization's employees can be devastating. It sends the anti-excellence message. By seeing their less-than-excellent work being sold to customers, employees learn that compromising their standards is acceptable.

Destroying guitars and sacrificing revenue from flawed products may be costly in the short term, but any organization committed to excellence must take such measures. The alternative, mediocrity, is worse. Organizations that seek true long-term loyalty from customers must deliver that same level of commitment. No excuses, including offering discounts, will matter. Organizations are either committed to excellence and the continued improvement of product and service standards, or they are not. Product and service excellence are more than just buzzwords or nice ideas; they serve as a competitive differentiator and strategic advantage.

Product and service excellence can also serve as a means to obtain a higher price for products and services. At Gibson, prices had been declining 20 percent a year and to the astonishment of employees, Henry not only raised prices, in some cases, he doubled them. Yet, even with a dramatic increase in price, volume continued to increase. By offering an exceptional, uncompromised product that delighted customers, Gibson was able to raise prices significantly and have customers reaffirm their conviction in the value delivered by their premium price products. Ultimately, customers rewarded excellence.

While Henry states that the chainsaw process continues to this day, he points out that the pile of broken guitars is much smaller. By sending the message that only perfection would be accepted, he has not only raised the quality of his company's guitars, but the production and service standards of his employees. After all, no employee wants to see the results of his laborious efforts being destroyed by a chainsaw. Yet Henry knew that employing harsh and somewhat theatrical measures were necessary to shake up his company. By keeping a watchful eye over the program, he made sure that his company's commitment to perfection would remain intact.

How do you tolerate less than excellence performance? What message do your employees receive when seeing their flawed products being sold anyway? Do you allow mediocrity into your organization while touting the message of excellence? As a rule of thumb, if you are willing to sell mediocrity to your customers, do not expect excellence from your employees. In a place where good enough is accepted, employees will not strive for excellence. As with all commitments, if dedication does not go up, it naturally goes down. This is a compromise that no company can afford to make.

Wrenching Customers Away from the Competition

Managing a hardware store is a physically demanding job, especially in August. Between answering questions, helping customers find what they need, managing a store full of employees, and keeping the paperwork up-to-date, there is little time to relax. When the time comes to close the door and go home, most store managers are ready to get off their feet and avoid having to solve any problems for a couple of hours.

But don't tell that to Frank, owner of Ace Hardware in Phoenix, Arizona. Just as he was about to close his store one summer night, he saw someone standing outside the shop looking in, desperately staring into the store. So, Frank unlocked the store and took the time to listen: Something had gone wrong with the lawn sprinklers, and water was pouring onto the man's yard. Frank asked a few questions but realized quickly that the man was—pardon the pun—in over his head.

Following a long day at work, some store managers will wash their hands of the customer's problems. They already have plans for what to do in the evening. The last thing they need is to extend their workday without pay. But Frank was different. He knew excellence is not completed until the customer is happy. His customer did not need tools or advice; he needed his problem resolved. He needed nothing less than excellence.

No problem. Frank went back into the store, collected all the tools and supplies he would need (without even stopping to ring them up), and followed the customer home to fix the leak. Thirty minutes later, the problem was solved, the homeowner was overjoyed, and Polimene's Ace Hardware had earned another lifetime customer.

When I first read this story in the *Franchise Times* (October 2005 edition), I was intrigued. The problem the customer faced clearly went beyond the need for tools. But Frank made a Daily Choice to focus on the impact of his actions. His customer did not need the tools; he needed the problem solved. Frank got that. Although he could have easily referred the customer to a plumber, the reality was that it was Frank who was presented with the customer's challenge. Frank took it personally. It was *his* opportunity for excellence. He looked at the challenge and saw a possibility: He saw an opportunity to help someone and an opportunity to make an impact. Frank did not see the customer's problem as a burden, despite being tired after a long day, but as a privilege. It was this commitment to excellence that encouraged him to delay his evening plans and help one more customer.

Excellence for Frank is measured one customer at a time. Frank knew that his customer needed a complete solution to his problem. That was the definition of excellence and that is what he delivered. When you engage with your customer, does your experience solve a problem or provide tools and let the customer take care of himself? Do you address the bigger picture or just your narrow definition of customer needs? This is exactly why we define excellence as judged by the recipient. Often, we claim excellence, but it is by our own terms. Those terms are often narrow, easy to achieve, and may ignore the big picture or the complete problem of our customers. It is a common mistake when excellence is self-centric and not customer-centric. How do you define excellence? Who defines the problem you solve: you or your customer?

Team Excellence or the Gifts Keep on Coming

This is a sad story with very happy ending. "Heather," an American guest, arrived at the Le Centre Sheraton Montreal for a convention. As part of her leisure activities, she traveled three hours each way to Mont Tremblant to do some shopping. Heather was delighted with what she found and purchased special T-shirts for her kids, chocolate, candles, and a teakettle, among many other things. Excited, Heather returned to her hotel room. She emptied all the shopping bags and consolidated her gifts in a big garbage bag, which she inadvertently placed next to the garbage can.

While she was at the convention the next day, Heather's room was cleaned. The maid noticed the large garbage bag next to the garbage can and decided to throw it away with the rest of the garbage. Her commitment to cleaning was never compromised. Not even a big garbage bag would deter her from making sure her rooms are spotless and ready to please the guests. Upon returning to her room, Heather was horrified to find out that her precious gifts were gone.

It was an honest mistake. After all, she had left her gifts in a garbage bag next to the garbage can. Heather should have been more careful. Enter team excellence. To the people at Le Centre Sheraton in Montreal, excuses and fault sharing are not the way to delight guests. The question of blame was not an issue at all. "We have to fix the mistake. We must assume complete responsibility," was the immediate reaction of Michel Giguere, the hotel's general manager. According to Michel, not much thinking was required. It was a gut reaction to simply do what was right for the guest.

But here was the next challenge. What was the right thing to do? Some would try to compensate Heather for her lost gifts and solve the problem this way. It would be pretty considerate, and they would bear a financial loss as a result of compensating the guest. But this was not enough for Michel and his staff. Michel decided to repurchase and replace the lost articles. Michel asked his assistant Marie to sit down with the guest and document each lost gift. From color and sizes of the T-shirts to the design of the teakettle, Marie spent more than an hour documenting the original purchases.

In the meantime, Michel also asked Maria Bentivegna, a dedicated concierge who is a member of Les Clefs d'Or Canada, an international concierge association, to pitch in as well. Her commitment to her guests was always absolute, and this time was not different. Maria agreed to travel to Mont Tremblant on her day off and spend the day shopping for the American guest. Even though she was offered a taxi, she refused and took the three-hour bus ride to get to the same stores where the American guest had shopped. Maria followed the written instructions from Marie and purchased a replacement for each of the gifts. On several occasions, she had to contact Marie directly to clarify the details to make sure she purchased the exact item the guest originally bought. It was a long process, and almost made Maria miss the last bus back, but her commitment was that strong.

Excellence was very personal to her. She drew her satisfaction from solving the problem. She knows that difficult times are the highest test of a commitment to excellence.

When I asked Maria why she accepted such a task, to go on her day off and shop for the guest, she simply replied, "I love my job. This is what I do. I love helping tourists and having them come back."

The American guest was amazed by this commitment to excellence and followed up with a letter indicating that Michel, Marie, and Maria redefined hospitality as we know it. And she was probably right. All they did is follow their natural commitment to excellence; they treated others just as they wish they would have been treated in such a situation. Although the mistake that caused the problem was an honest one and clearly not the fault of the hotel, none of that mattered. If you are in the business of excellence, you are in the business of delighting customers.

The final result of your actions, as reflected in the eyes of your customers, is what matters the most. The customer is the ultimate judge.

Sometimes it takes more than one person to create excellence. Michel needed a small team to create excellence for Heather. And he found them right away, because his was not a hotel of individuals but of a group of people unified by a mission and a commitment to excellence in hospitality. By creating the culture of excellence in the hotel, he could assemble a like-minded team in matter of minutes. Michel managed to institutionalize excellence so that, in the moment of truth, with guest in need, he had his team excellence ready to get the job done.

How many people would you be able to assemble for such a performance? Do they all visualize excellence in the same way as you do? How far would they be willing to go? You cannot wait for the moment of truth to present itself to know the answer. The efforts to build a culture of excellence today will turn the moment of truth into a natural excellence performance. These moments of truth are your true test of commitment to excellence. Practicing for them is what you must do every day.

CHAPTER 14

Just Imagine …
Then Make
It Happen

Imagine a company where every employee demonstrates a top level of responsibility and delivers the excellence we've seen in the previous chapters. Imagine a company where the heroes of these stories work together. Just imagine the impact, superior performance, competitive advantage, and customer loyalty such a company would generate. Imagine a company where the standard is defined based on the recipient and not by adhering to internal process. Imagine a company where managers take the lead in permitting employees to perform and stop making nuisance decisions, such as "To tie or not to tie." In this company, managers celebrate mistakes (the right mistakes, of course). Managers are in charge of enabling excellence, removing obstacles, and focusing on letting employees make the right Daily Choices for excellence every day. Imagine a company where employees focus on wow and won't settle for consistency, where the organization's assets are defined in terms of employee Daily Choices and not process optimization, and where employees take ownership of the complete problem of the recipient, whether an internal or external customer. Imagine a company where employees rise to the occasion during tough times and do for others what they would like others to do for them. Imagine a company where "seconds" are banned and are destroyed with a chainsaw because excellence is the only rule: It's excellence or nothing.

Wouldn't you want to work there? I know I would. It would be an honor and privilege to work with these great people who are committed to excellence. You almost know that their commitment to excellence will affect you. Excellence would be contagious in such a place.

In many ways, you have no choice but to imagine this organization because your competitors are pushing the envelope faster and higher. Your customers demand this high level of excellence and refuse to accept anything less. This excellence is possible, as we saw in the diverse stories told in the previous chapters. You need to start by making the choice. Then, you need to make sure all these everyday heroes (or those equally committed to excellence) work with you.

Enabling excellence in your organization is not an *option* anymore. Your commitment to excellence must be absolute because it is a matter of differentiation and growth. It is a matter of making you and your organization indispensable. To stay competitive, you can no longer afford random acts of excellence conducted by a few individuals who are the exception to the rule. You need excellence to happen every day, by every employee, in every Daily Choice. Excellence needs to be the rule, not the exception. Following the Six Sigma formula drives consistency through the optimized processes delivered by many organizations. Excellence through people is still a rare virtue, commanding attention and premium. But by working with your people as the prime differentiators of the business, excellence will become the way to unleash the power of their innovation, caring, and commitment. It is only through their own choice that they will deliver their best. The paycheck will definitely not do it alone.

I am confident that the commitment to excellence appears in your organization's statement of mission and values. (Who would not place it there? It sounds good as an aspiration.) But as our study indicates, the problem is not with intentions or fancy slogans. The problem is with the actual behaviors that are supposed to fulfill the promise. Delivering excellence will not happen because you listed it on a poster. It will not become a reality because you sent a memo titled "Leading Through Excellence." Building an organization capable of delivering excellence is a disciplined way of thinking that requires departure from the old ways and insists on adopting new practices to support excellence enablement.

Your competitiveness is defined not through the number of Six Sigma processes you developed but through the millions of Daily Choices your employees make every day. Through these choices, they decided to deliver excellence and strengthen the organization. By succumbing to a focus on processes, your organization will be weaker and less competitive. This is not a question of better processes. It is a question of what creates the difference: the process or the people. What serves what? Are people subservient to processes, or are processes just the tools to help people perform? Understanding this difference is crucial to understanding why we are not delivering excellence already.

Redefining and reframing excellence as a daily occurrence and not a rare lifetime achievement is important to shifting away from the Excellence Myth. Excellence belongs to everyone who wants to deliver it. That means it is you who chooses to unleash this power for excellence. Your employees *are* capable of excellence, but they may simply choose *not* to deliver it in *your* organization in every act. They will take their excellence elsewhere.

Start with yourself. Your employees follow your actions, not your words. Make yourself the symbol of everyday excellence. Demonstrate your commitment through your Daily Choices. Your leadership will create an excellence-enabling environment. You will build both the willingness and capacity to deliver excellence. This excellence translates into innovation, caring, better decision making, and, ultimately, a stronger, more competitive organization. Excellence cannot be forced. Your people need to want to do it. It is treading on the domain of your employees' personal choice. A simple choice made by a willing employee will make all the difference. At the end of the day, your organizations are *only* as strong as those Daily Choices.

Are You Ready to Deliver Excellence?

Imagine a devoted fan of Tiger Woods. The fan is so dedicated that he spends the majority of his free time scanning every piece of information published about the golfer anywhere around the world. He collects this information in neatly arranged albums. He spends hours watching golf tournaments in which Tiger plays; he can recite by heart Tiger's performance records throughout the years. The fan has an impressive collection of books, magazines, press clippings, and other paraphernalia that qualify him as the world's expert on Tiger Woods. He even met the golf pro several times and has autographed photos and golf balls from him. What are the chances that this fan will win the next PGA golf championship? Would you bet your money on this fan? Probably not.

In excellence, as in sports, knowledge does not define your performance capacity. You can spend your life studying all the theoretical aspects of a certain sport, but unless you get out and play it, abstract knowledge is useless. All you have accumulated is a theoretical knowledge that was never tested in real life. So yes, you may study excellence books all your life, but practicing excellence is the real deal. Excellence is not a matter of expert knowledge; it is a habit. The more you practice by making Daily Choices for it, the better your impact and results. This is it. It's show time! You need to do it.

The Talmud teaches us that a person who saves one soul is equal in importance to a person who saves the entire world. The reason, the Talmud explains, is because every person is equal to a whole world.

Every human being is a whole world because every person can make an impact and change the world. Every person is a whole world full of challenges, problems, difficulties, aspiration, dreams, and hopes. Every person can advance their dreams, minimize their problems and challenges, and become more whole overall through the help of people like you who select excellence. There are many recipients waiting for your excellence every day everywhere.

In every Daily Choice, we have an opportunity to save the whole world by saving one person's world. By viewing every person as a unique world, unlike any other in the *whole* world, we can see the value of saving or making an impact on each person. Every person is a uniquely different world with a unique mission *in* this world. By assisting the other, we save their world and allow them to make their contribution to ours. By making the choice for excellence, we embrace the opportunity to save a person, be of assistance, and make his life easier or more enjoyable.

As I was developing the concept of this book, I spoke to a friend about the premise and then asked the following question: "What if I invented a pill you can swallow, and it immediately transformed you into the excellence domain—would you take it? Can we take a pill and create a short cut to excellence?" As I expected, his answer was "No." He would not take the short cut. To his own surprise, he realized that certain things in life do not mean the same to you if you try to achieve them by taking a short cut. Excellence is one of them. If you attempt to buy your way into achieving excellence and avoid the hard work and effort associated with actually doing it, you miss achieving excellence. The results do not mean the same without the effort.

This is difficult to admit in a world where we pay our way out of dealing with many responsibilities. We buy time by paying others to do things we should to do. And yet, here it is: Achieving excellence is the one thing we probably will *not* try to buy our way out of or take a short cut to realize. The beauty of assisting others is not the same without the effort associated with the act of doing it. You need to be out there to experience the thrill. You need to be part of the experience and not a passive observer to make things happen and enjoy the thrill. Reading or observing an experience does not equal actually living it. We often associate success and gratification with effort. Anything achieved quickly can be lost just as quickly. We tend to cherish and appreciate whatever we labor for, and the larger the effort, the greater the appreciation.

Lifelong Pursuit of Excellence

When Glenn Holland joined the faculty of JFK High School in 1964, it was a temporary gig. He was teaching music with the intention of saving enough to pursue his life passion of composing an amazing opus. He did his job in order to pursue his lifelong dream. Teaching was just a way to make a living. But life had its own dynamics: His wife became pregnant unexpectedly and other life events forced the temporary gig to become a 31-year career. As he retired, he reflected on his life and the missed opportunity to purse his life's real dream. But as the final scene in the movie *Mr. Holland's Opus* shows, he accomplished an amazing life's work. His students gathered to pay homage to the teacher who inspired them through his devotion to music.

Mr. Holland's Opus is one of my favorite movies. I am always touched by the final scene as Glenn Holland (played by Richard Dreyfuss) gets to review his life's accomplishments through the success and growth of the students he impacted. He might not have achieved the legendary definition of excellence as a once-in-a-lifetime event or creation, but he did it through everyday excellence. Every day, he brought his devotion and passion to music and shared it with others. He focused on making an impact on others and created an amazing, colorful fabric of success and excellence by reaching out to one student at a time. It is rare for a person to actually see the accumulated power of all his Daily Choices of excellence, as Mr. Holland was able to see in that final scene. That is why I find this scene so powerful.

If we each make a mental note of all the people that we touch every day and choose to deliver excellence and not mediocrity, then our picture will be just as powerful over time. Our Daily Choices create accumulated excellence and impact the world more than a one-time discovery. If you haven't seen *Mr. Holland's Opus*, watch it. If you have seen it, watch it again. The movie will remind you that despite all the challenges, we can make an impact, we can choose excellence, and, if we do that, the accumulated power of our Daily Choices will be enormous. Excellence may be found in the most unexpected places. Life is what happens to you while you're making other plans. Excellence happens in the actions we take, not the plans we make, unless those plans become actions. At the moment of the Daily Choice, it is difficult to see the accumulated impact. But on reflection, over time, as Glenn Holland discovers, the impact becomes overwhelmingly amazing. That is the power of disciplined Daily Choices for excellence with full focus on taking responsibility and helping others.

Only 15 Minutes of Fame?

Andy Warhol was credited with saying that everyone will have his 15 minutes of fame. (In Internet time, some argue that fame shrank to 15 seconds.) When I pondered on this statement, I found it very depressing. Is that all we have to strive for in this world—15 minutes of fame? What about the rest of our lives? Are we supposed to spend half of our lives in expectation of the desired 15 minutes and the other half reminiscing about them?

What if we could make every day of our lives 15 minutes of fame? What if every day could matter and make us famous? What if every Daily Choice could give us 15 minutes of fame? If we just reframe our definition of fame, change it from that of admiration of screaming crowds who do not know us to fame among those who are affected by our actions. If we do that, we can make every day, every single *choice* our 15 minutes of fame. And if we miss it one day, we get another chance the next day. Every Daily Choice for excellence becomes our opportunity for another 15 minutes of fame.

The alternative is simply too pathetic for words. To live 99.9 percent of your life either in expectation of a one-time event or in memory of a great achievement is a waste of your life. It is a waste of the excellence potential you have. This way of thinking belongs with the dinosaurs and the Excellence Myth, where we define excellence as a rare, never-to-happen-again event. We can live better than that. We can rise above sorry excuses for procedures and processes that hold us back. We can create our own life as an endless series of famous minutes.

Sorry, Andy Warhol. I will take 15 minutes of everyday fame over the once-in-a-lifetime allocation you envisioned. Instead of searching for once-in-a-lifetime flashes of fame, let's create them every day. Let us create excellence every day, excellence that generates fame for every action we do. Everything we do should be so superior that it merits the full 15 minutes. By doing so, we will one day look back, just as Mr. Holland did, and discover that our lives were richer, filled with excellence and countless minutes of fame, as reflected in the eyes of the people who matter: the recipients of our performance.

It's Showtime

It's time to turn our focus back to excellence. It is time to remove the distractions, like our attitude of inaptitude. It is time to kick the habit and recover from our addiction to Dilbertism. It is time to regain our competitiveness by focusing our efforts on excellence. All the cynical jokes might be temporarily funny, but they are damaging—no, devastating—in the long term. Like a virus attacking an organism, these jokes can erode our capacity for excellence. You must re-establish your conviction. To face emerging competition, you must reshape your approach to the battle. Going to war with a defeatist attitude (which is exactly what the attitude of inaptitude does to us) is a recipe for failure. Many of us who suffer the attitude of inaptitude do not even show up to the battlefield. Instead, we forfeit this battle in the name of our incompetent boss and moron CEO.

Whatever your role, your power is enormous. You hold the ability to impact others in your hands. Consider your power as a call-center representative who makes 10,000 Daily Choices a year. It is vast. You touch 10,000 customers in a year. So is the power of the receptionist in the hotel, the salesperson in a store, the IT person, or the manufacturing worker. Your choices for excellence make a significant difference to the customers you serve and the organizations you join. With your peers, you can make a difference for millions of customers every year and create powerful differentiation that no competitor will be able to match.

We have this power, but we must regain the conviction. We must redefine excellence and our organization's strength, not from the viewpoint of our market value, stock price, or brand equity. We must define excellence as the accumulation of what we do every day. Our Daily Choices for excellence will determine the power, strength, and competitiveness of our organization. Our company is the total of the excellence actions of each and every one of our people, not the total of our processes or any other abstract asset. Processes, tools, information, brand, and assets are all vehicles to achieve organizational excellence. The better the tools are, the more effective the information, the better the performance of the employees. But let's not confuse the tool and the person. Without people, all these tools are useless. You breathe life into an organization's excellence simply by practicing excellence.

Be Originally You

True excellence and impact performance stem from originality and authenticity. In the culture of admiring the legends (real or false), we tend to overemphasize the legends and underemphasize ourselves. We create an intimidating frame of reference for ourselves that discourages us from actually trying to make excellence happen. We belittle our capabilities in light of the towering top achievers we admire. We ignore our own existence and downplay our capabilities to make room within us for the admiration of others. Our actions then soon follow as we imitate the legends we admire as opposed to creating our own voice. We define ourselves by our weaknesses and not by our own strengths. We compensate for our weaknesses by admiring others. I call it "living on the fringe of life," or living in someone else's life.

If we sit on the fringe of life, we stare at the performance on the main stage of our legend's life, a performance conducted by our subject of admiration. We will never dare to set foot on stage. After all, we will never live up to their excellence capabilities. At best, we can buy the T-shirts at the end of the show: been there, done that, got the T-shirt. But life and excellence are not about T-shirts. Life is not about the winning of the consolation prize. It is about being the top performer on our own world stage. Our heroes have their own skills and capabilities—as well as their own weaknesses (believe it or not). They live their lives accordingly. You need to live yours, playing on center stage, according to your own excellence capacity. But you will never get to do it if you constantly compare yourself to someone who is completely different from you.

We were all created differently. As our fingerprints and DNA illustrate, we are all different people who are uniquely crafted and authentically different. There is something unnatural about trying to imitate someone else's life. It simultaneously creates both a void and redundancy. When you try to make your life and your legend's life the same, one of you becomes redundant. And your own unique life and your excellence go missing, which creates a void in the world. Each of us is powerful and unique, which is needed in this world. If you try to be someone else or live another person's life, you will become redundant and merely a pale imitation of the original. At the same time, you will leave the world lacking the uniqueness you were created to give.

Viktor Frankel, a Holocaust survivor, developed his psychological theory while he was incarcerated in a Nazi concentration camp, facing death every day. In his book *Man's Search for Meaning*, he discusses the refusal to accept that we are victims of fate. His book discusses the fact that despite all the difficulties, no one can take away a certain freedom from every human being, which is the freedom to respond. Regardless of the circumstances, we all have the freedom to respond whether as victims of fate or as capable people who can make things happen. You can treat yourself as an object or subject. You can assume helplessness or hopefulness. You can demonstrate paralysis or take action. You can focus on tasks or impact. The freedom is yours to choose how to respond to the challenges presented to you. Be yourself. Be who you are and play on your center stage.

The More You Give, the More You Have

Power is measured by divisions. Influence is measured by multiplication. It is all a matter of perspective. When viewing life as a zero-sum game, you quickly reach the conclusion that the more you give, the less you have. When sharing a cake, the problem is well-illustrated. The bigger the slices you give to others, the smaller your slice will be. But if we choose to view the world from the perspective of influence and not power, the results of sharing change dramatically. Take the same cake. When lighting the candles, you quickly notice that when you light the other candles with one lit candle, you achieve greater light without losing anything. The lit candle does not lose anything by giving light to other candles. The same principle applies to smiles. The more you spread your smile, the more smiling people will be around you and the greater the total sum of smiling. You lose absolutely nothing by smiling and triggering smiles in others.

When sharing and delivering excellence is viewed as coming from a rare reservoir of excellence that is at risk of depletion (from a sense of *lacking)*, we tend to minimize it. We fear that the more we give, the less we will have left for ourselves. We treat excellence as a scarce power. But when viewing excellence as influence, we recognize that sharing in abundance does not shrink our capacity for excellence, but rather, it creates more around us. By sharing more in abundance, we obtain more through reciprocal excellence given to us by others. Giving excellence becomes having more.

True giving, despite the common perception, is a matter of influence and not power. The more you give, the more you have. Spreading excellence around you creates a more nurturing environment for excellence. This is true in your personal and professional lives. One act of excellence brings more. As you develop the excellence habit, more Daily Choices are made more easily. You will develop your capacity to deliver even greater excellence next time. The more you give excellence, the richer your excellence will be. The sacrifices and efforts you have to put forth to create excellence will be rewarded with more excellence around you and within you. Your reservoir of excellence will become richer, stronger, and more capable.

I Think I Can ...

You think you can deliver excellence? Well, that is a good start. But the crucial question is not whether you can. With your unique skills and experience, you are more than capable of delivering excellence in your interest areas. The crucial question is whether you *want* to. To reach superior performance, you need to *want* to do it. The commitment to excellence has to come from your heart, not your head. Thinking is a logical process based on facts and assessments, but it doesn't necessarily lead to action. Wanting is the fast track to action, and it comes from a different part of you. Wanting is subjective and is the result of your personal choice. Many people might share the same capabilities to deliver excellence. But only those who choose to use them will deliver excellence.

Wanting is the willingness to do it because it is worthy of doing. It is a very personal choice; it is a personal commitment to promote a personally important cause. I believe that if you have read the book this far, the miracle of excellence performance is within you. You read more because you wanted to be inspired and encouraged. It starts with a simple Daily Choice. Start the journey, and the more Daily Choices you make, the stronger and more capable of excellence you will be. It is a journey. It is ultimately the choice to live life by excellence and not by excuses.

A common excuse for not delivering excellence is the pseudo-humility trap. We think that by minimizing our goals, we stay humble and satisfy a smaller appetite. We do not want to overshadow others by making big things happen. After all, it will make them look bad. But this is just another excuse. This pseudo-humility does not help anyone. All we do is lower our expectations and become unhappy, like many other people who are not fulfilling their potential and living up to their capacity for excellence. It is an excuse not to raise our sights to higher goals and possibilities for excellence.

This is not the time to be humble. Others may argue (aka, excuse) that excellence demands too much effort. In reality, you may actually only invest the same amount of energy, time, and effort as you do today. Instead of investing energy in reaffirming the Excellence Myth and convincing yourself you cannot, use these special resources to build your excellence capacity and deliver superior performance. It is more a matter of how we direct our efforts as opposed to more vs. less. The time and effort we spend denying our capabilities while reading cynical Internet jokes can simply be redirected to create positive outcomes and lead to excellence performance. It is your choice to make.

The fulfillment of our excellence capacity is both a duty and a privilege. Denying your capacity for excellence means denying the world your best. It also means denying yourself the greatness of living up to the maximum of your excellence capacity, growing personally, and professionally with each Daily Choice, and knowing that you make a difference. Make a difference to a whole world, a world of one person in hope or millions in need. Either way, you make a world of difference through your choices.

Higher and Higher

Did you ever see an Olympic pole vault competition? If you think about it, it is one of the strangest competitions you can witness. Competitors keep on winning until they fail. Until the final athlete fails to make it over the bar, the competition is not over. Unlike other sports where there are clear winners and losers, in the pole vault, you keep on trying until you fail. Even the gold medalist must fail before earning his top prize. In fact, the winner of the competition is the one who failed at the highest level.

Imagine a pole vaulter jumping over the bar and then deciding to go home. "I am very happy with my performance. It is good enough for me," he might say. That, of course, would be totally unacceptable, and that's not how the competition works. The pole vaulter's coach will argue with him to keep trying. "What is the point? I will fail eventually," the athlete might respond to the coach. "You must keep on trying because it is the only way you will know how high you can go before you fail" would most likely be the response from the coach.

In the pole vault, you do not settle for good enough. You keep on trying to greater heights. You cannot just quit after one try and be satisfied with your performance. You keep on reaching higher, knowing that at some point, you will fail. But the attempts to reach higher will also lead you to heights you did not know you could reach without continuing to try. As paradoxical as it sounds, you will never know how high you can reach until you reached your point of failure. (Remember, it might be your point of failure today, but your victory point tomorrow.)

The same principle applies to excellence. You must keep on trying, and you must try to reach higher. Always raise the bar on your own performance. Believe that you can reach higher than what you can imagine. What was excellence yesterday will be old news today. The excellence bar is always moving higher and higher. Sometimes the bar is raised by others' performances; other times, it is raised by your own performance that sets new records of excellence. But accepting yesterday's excellence as good enough for today is succumbing to complacency. Today, you need to create new excellence standards. It is part of the ever-evolving journey upward toward new heights of excellence. By default, if we do not reach higher, we sink lower. There is no standing still. Raise the bar on your excellence achievements. Just like the pole vault athlete, you do not know in advance how high you can reach. You know what you have achieved and how high you *have* reached. But you do not know how high you *can* reach. Unless, of course, you make the attempt and jump.

It is not a matter of retrospective analysis, it is simply a matter of being proactive. As it is with the pole vault, if you do not attempt, someone else will. If it does not happen in this competition, it will happen in the next. The new record will be set. The only question is, will it be you who breaks the old record and ushers in the new one? The more you try, the better your chances. The higher you reach, the greater your chances are to get there. Is it scary? Sure. Are you confident you can achieve it? Nothing is certain. The option of failure is still possible (and if we follow

Afterword:
Moving Forward

Now what? Now is action time. Excellence is a journey full of actions. You must keep yourself inspired and motivated, and this book is just the beginning—a launching pad in your excellence career.

In the book, I have presented a sampling of stories and practices: There are countless other everyday stories of excellence that can and will inspire us to deliver superior performance. As you come across stories that inspire you, share them. As you make Daily Choices that impact someone's world and life, make a record of them. Keep this book and your commitment to excellence alive by adding your personal examples of success and excellence, both those you have delivered to others and those delivered to you.

Keep yourself motivated. Create a personal legacy by making amazing personal Daily Choices. Create a personal guidebook you can share with others. Make excellence *live* in your life every day.

Share your stories and experiences at www.ExcellenceEveryDay.com.

About the Author

Lior Arussy is an author, visionary, consultant, and creative catalyst who specializes in helping firms create delightful customer experiences and execute profitable customer strategies. He is the founder and president of Strativity Group, Inc., which advises Global 2000 companies and emerging businesses around the world.

Lior's clients include Nokia, Computer Associates, SAP, American Management Association, Seagate Technology, Honeywell, Siemens, Lockheed Martin, Wyeth, University of Pennsylvania, FedEx, CATIC, and Nordea.Prior to establishing Strativity Group, he held executive positions at Hewlett-Packard and other companies.

Lior's syndicated column "Focus: Customer" reaches more than 600,000 readers worldwide every month. He is the author of four books, including *Passionate & Profitable: Why Customer Strategies Fail and 10 Steps to Do Them Right!* (Wiley, 2005). He has published more than 50 articles in publications around the world, including the *Harvard Business Review.*

Lior's accomplishments have been recognized by leading analysts and media firms including ABC, the *Wall Street Journal, Financial Times, The Times of London,* and the Gartner Group. For his thought leadership and contributions to the Customer Relationship Management (CRM) industry, Lior received *CRM Magazine*'s 2003 "Influential Leaders" award and served as a juror for Fast Company's 2005 Customer First Awards.

Lior received his undergraduate degree from Case Western Reserve University and his MBA from Weatherhead School of Management.

More Great Books from Information Today, Inc.

Designing the Digital Experience

How to Use Experience Design Tools and Techniques to Build Websites Customers Love

By David Lee King

Today's marketers and site designers can harness the power of "experience design" to help customers quickly find information, make purchases, or participate. *Library Journal* "Mover & Shaker" David Lee King explains the concepts behind designing digital experiences, describes a range of new tools and techniques, and shares experience design best practices.

224 pp/softbound/ISBN 978-0-910965-83-5 $39.95

Laughing at the CIO

A Parable and Prescription for IT Leadership

By Bob Boiko

Through his modern-day fable of information technology gone awry, Bob Boiko shows execs and tech staff alike how to harness the "I" in "IT" to become leaders by making measurable movement toward strategic goals. Boiko's business parable leads to a set of concrete methods you can use to create IT strategy and action in your organization. Whether or not you are a CIO, if you recognize the power of information and have the desire to be an information leader, this book and Web-based ebook will show you the way.

224 pp/softbound & ebook/ISBN 978-0-910965-78-1 $29.95
Ebook only/ISBN 978-1-57387-946-0 $29.95

CRM in Real Time
Empowering Customer Relationships

By Barton J. Goldenberg

This guide to customer relationship management (CRM) shows how the right mix of people, process, and technology can help firms achieve a superior level of customer satisfaction, loyalty, and new business. *CRM in Real Time* covers a full range of critical issues, including integration challenges and security concerns, and illuminates CRM's key role in the 24/7/365 real-time business revolution.

384 pp/softbound/ISBN 978-0-910965-80-4 $39.95

Smart Services
Competitive Information Strategies, Solutions and Success Stories for Service Businesses

By Deborah C. Sawyer

Here is the first book to focus specifically on the competitive information needs of service-oriented firms. Deborah C. Sawyer illuminates the many forms of competition in service businesses, identifies the most effective information resources for competitive intelligence (CI), and provides a practical framework for identifying and studying competitors.

256 pp/softbound/ISBN 978-0-910965-56-9 $29.95